D1253348

Consensus Politics from Attlee to Major

Making Contemporary Britain Series

General Editor: Anthony Seldon
Consultant Editor: Peter Hennessy

Published

Northern Ireland since 1968
Paul Arthur and Keith Jeffrey
The Prime Minister since 1945
James Barber
British General Elections since 1945
David Butler
The British Economy since 1945
Alec Cairncross
Britain and the Suez Crisis
David Carlton
The End of the British Empire
John Darwin
British Defence since 1945
Michael Dockrill
Britain and the Falklands War
Lawrence Freedman
Britain and European Integration
since 1945
Stephen George
Consensus Politics from Attlee to
Major
Dennis Kavanagh and Peter Morris
The Politics of Immigration
Zig Layton-Henry
Women in Britain since 1945
Jane Lewis
Britain and the Korean War
Callum Macdonald
Culture in Britain since 1945
Arthur Marwick
Crime and Criminal Justice since
1945
Terence Morris
The British Press and Broadcasting
since 1945
Colin Seymour-Ure

Third Party Politics since 1945
John Stevenson
The Trade Union Question in British
Politics
Robert Taylor
British Science and Politics since
1945
Thomas Wilkie
British Public Opinion
Robert M. Worcester

Forthcoming

British Industry since 1945
Margaret Ackrill
The Conservative Party since 1945
John Barnes
The British Monarchy
Robert Blackburn
The Labour Party since 1945
Brian Brivati and Andrew Thomas
Electoral Change since 1945
Ivor Crewe and Pippa Norris
Religion in Britain
Grace Davie
British Politics since 1945
Peter Dorey
British Social Policy since 1945
Howard Glennerster
Sport in Britain since 1945
Richard Holt and Tony Mason
Parliament since 1945
Philip Norton
The Civil Service since 1945
Kevin Theakston
Terrorism since 1945
Paul Wilkinson

Consensus Politics from Attlee to Major

Second edition

Dennis Kavanagh and Peter Morris

BLACKWELL
Oxford UK & Cambridge USA

First published 1989
Second edition published 1994 (twice)

Blackwell Publishers, the publishing imprint of Basil Blackwell Ltd
108 Cowley Road
Oxford OX4 1JF, UK

Basil Blackwell Inc.
238 Main Street
Cambridge, Massachusetts 02142
USA

British Library Cataloguing in Publication Data
A CIP catalogue record for this book is available from the British Library.

Library of Congress Cataloging-in-Publication Data
Kavanagh, Dennis.
    Consensus politics from Attlee to Major/Dennis Kavanagh and Peter Morris. – 2nd ed.
        p. cm. – (Making contemporary Britain)
    Rev. ed. of: Consensus politics from Attlee to Thatcher. 1989.
    Includes bibliographical references and index.
    ISBN 0–631–19228–X (acid-free paper)
    1. Great Britain – Economic policy – 1945– 2. Great Britain – Social policy – 1979– 3. Great Britain – Politics and government – 1945–
4. Great Britain – Foreign relations – 1945– 5. Consensus (Social sciences) I. Morris, Peter. II. Kavanagh, Dennis. Consensus politics from Attlee to Thatcher. III. Title. IV. Series.
HC256.5.K34   1994
338.941–dc20   93–48395
                                                                                                                    CIP

Printed in Great Britain by Athenæum Press Ltd., Gateshead, Tyne & Wear.

Contents

To Monica and Rosie

General Editor's Preface

The Institute of Contemporary British History's series, *Making Contemporary Britain*, is aimed at school students, undergraduates and others interested in learning more about topics in post-war British history. In the series, authors are less concerned with breaking new ground than with presenting clear and balanced overviews of the state of knowledge on each of the topics.

The ICBH, which produces the series, was founded in October 1986 with the objective of promoting the study at every level of British history since 1945. To that end it publishes books and a quarterly journal, *Contemporary Record*, it organizes seminars and conferences for sixth-formers, undergraduates, researchers and teachers of post-war history, and it runs a number of research programmes and other activities.

A central belief of the ICBH's work is that post-war history is too often neglected in British schools, institutes of higher education and beyond. The ICBH acknowledges the validity of the arguments against the study of recent history, notably the problems of bias and of overly subjective teaching and writing, and the difficulties of perspective. But it believes that the values of studying post-war history outweigh the drawbacks, and that the health and future of a liberal democracy require that its citizens know more about the most recent past of their country than the limited knowledge possessed by British citizens, young and old, today. Indeed, the ICBH believes that the dangers of political indoctrination are higher when the young are *not* informed of the recent past of their country.

The thesis that a 'consensus' or broad agreement existed between both main parties on important areas of policy for much of the post-war period is not a new one: as early as February 1954 *The Economist* coined the word 'Butskellism' to refer to the continuity in economic policy between the Labour chancellor Hugh Gaitskell (1950–1) and the Conservative R. A. Butler (1951–5). The term 'consensus' began to achieve widespread currency following the publication in 1975 of Paul Addison's seminal *The Road to 1945*. By the 1980s, the term had become commonplace.

But not everyone accepts that a consensus occurred. Ben Pimlott (1988) is prime among the sceptics. He has argued that 'the consensus is a mirage, an illusion that rapidly fades the closer one gets to it.' To Pimlott, it is only from the perspective of the 1980s that there appears to have been harmony before; during the period 1945–79, he argues, the divisions were bitter and almost continuous. Politicians from both main parties never regarded themselves as belonging to a consensus.

Professor Dennis Kavanagh and Peter Morris pilot readers through the complete arguments over what the consensus in practice meant, the content of its five main 'planks', and the extent to which Margaret Thatcher has dismantled the consensus since coming to office in 1979. Combining the skills and methods of the political scientist and political historian, the authors produce a lucid and well-documented argment to show convincingly the nature and extent of the post-war consensus. In doing so, they serve to illuminate a large portion of post-war history, and to set the record of the Thatcher Government in its proper historical context.

The debate about the postwar consensus has not died with the departure of Mrs Thatcher. Quite the opposite: her political demise has given a new piquancy to the scholarly and popular discussion of the consensus idea in at least two ways. It is now possible to assess with a degree of hindsight exactly how far Mrs Thatcher did change the mould of postwar British politics. John Major's stewardship of Number 10, already longer than five of the postwar premiers, can also be brought into focus, and his policies scrutinized to see how far they are continuing on from those of Mrs Thatcher, starting out on a new course, or returning to the verities of the postwar consensus.

The second edition of this widely-read book is thus as important as it is timely.

Anthony Seldon

Preface

The writing of this book is based on two assumptions. The first is that there were discernible and significant continuities in many areas of British policy and political approach from the Attlee government to the mid-1970s. The second is that from the mid-1970s onwards, there has been a clear break with many of those continuities. In using the word 'consensus' to describe the policy mix of the post-war decades, we are aware of its limitations but remain convinced that it is a useful descriptive term. The five areas of public policy which we examine – the mixed economy, full employment, trade unions, welfare and foreign policy – could, of course, have been complemented by others, such as education and housing. But the five areas selected do form, in our opinion, the central planks of the post-war consensus. Our intention has been not to write five case studies, but to highlight some major themes of post-war British politics which make it possible to understand how an adversarial party system could coincide with broad areas of policy consensus. It is a contribution to the debate about the recent past and present state of British politics.

The idea of the book was suggested by Anthony Seldon. For comments on earlier versions we are grateful to Vernon Bogdanor, Peter Hennessy, Jane Kavanagh, John McClelland and Anthony Seldon. We also thank April Pidgeon for the cheerful and efficient way in which she has typed the manuscript.

Dennis Kavanagh, Peter Morris
Politics Department, Nottingham University

1 The Rise and Fall of Consensus Politics

Introduction

Consensus is a much used – some would say abused – word in British politics. It is an example (Eurocommunism is another) of a term that originated outside party political discourse and then became absorbed into it. The term acquired prominence in 1975 with the publication of Paul Addison's *The Road to 1945*. Addison argued that British politics since the First World War could be divided into two periods, which he labelled respectively the consensus of Baldwin and the consensus of Attlee. This did not mean that Stanley Baldwin and/or Clement Attlee singlehandedly created a set of principles and strategies by which British politics was organized; the idea was rather that each symbolized and became the focus of a set of ideas and conventions about the nature and scope of political – and particularly governmental – activity. They represented, in other words, a set of governing assumptions and expectations. Essentially, the hands-off approach that had characterized government's attitude towards the economy and society was replaced by a more dynamic and interventionist one. Addison saw the Second World War as a catalyst for the implementation of ideas that had been developed in the years before 1939.

The date of the publication of Addison's book is significant. It was a time when the consensus which he described was breaking down. Nineteen-seventy-five was the year in which Margaret Thatcher became leader of the Conservative Party and it also marked the last period of Labour government under a leadership that had gained its formative political experience in the period of the Attlee Government. Thus the consensus which Addison described as a historical fact became an issue within contemporary politics. Within a few years, the idea of consensus was promoted by Conservative dissidents or 'wets', unhappy with what they saw as Thatcherite radicalism, to describe a policy mix which they thought she had abandoned. Mrs Thatcher took up the challenge in a famous interview in 1981, in which she rejected, on grounds of political morality, the value of consensus politics: 'For me, consensus seems to be the process of abandoning all beliefs, principles, values and policies.' What happened on the right in British politics was mirrored on the left. As the Labour Party, particularly after 1979, moved sharply leftwards in both its domestic and foreign policies, those who resisted the change, often to the extent of leaving the party for the newly formed Social Democratic Party, did so in the name of the post-war consensus.

Addison was not the first scholar to describe British politics in terms of a consensus. It can, indeed, be argued that if consensus means a high level of agreement at both elite and popular level about the basic legitimacy of political institutions, then it has always existed in modern British politics. With the important exception of Ireland, debates over the form of regime, or the proper relationship between the different political institutions, have never occupied the place in modern British politics that they have elsewhere in Europe. The dominant role of traditional social elites has never been seriously threatened and religion has never been as divisive as in France or Italy, for example. Constitutional questions have of course formed part of the agenda of politics (reform of the House of Lords before 1914, the devolution issue in the 1970s), but they have not succeeded in destroying the constitutional framework – or the high regard in which it is held. After the second world war, the prestige of the constitution enabled Britain to export Westminster-type constitutions to many of her newly independent colonies.

The capacity of the system to absorb the challenge posed by the emergence of organized working class politics is perhaps the most famous example of this institutional consensus. Explanations for this absorption vary; but the fact that it undoubtedly occurred gave credence to the reassuring statement in 1927 of a former prime minister, Lord Balfour: 'Our whole political machinery presupposes a people so fundamentally at one that they can safely afford to bicker; and so sure of their own moderation that they are not dangerously disturbed by the never-ending din of political conflict.'

The absence of a 'revolutionary alternative' in British politics does not in itself prove that political debate and policy choices are carried out within a common set of assumptions, still less that there is total agreement. It may show, rather, the very elitist nature of the political process in Britain, the existence of a homogenous political class which has been able to determine the nature of the political agenda and exclude that of which it disapproves. The difficulty with this type of explanation, however, is that it fails to take account of the intensely partisan nature of political debate in Britain as well as the adversarial nature of party competition. Political discussion has never lacked passion, and debate between the parties has often been markedly antagonistic. It was precisely because competing party structures and loyalties were so strong that 'new ideas' had such difficulty in breaking through in the interwar years; and whatever else the Second World War may have done to British politics, it did nothing to weaken the stranglehold of the parties on policy implementation.

So if the term consensus is to be used to describe significant aspects of British politics in the period after 1945, it is important to be clear about the sense in which the word is being employed. Broadly speaking, it is used in two senses, apart from the agreement on political institution and procedures. One refers to a *style* of government characterized by institutionalized consultation between government and the major economic actors, including notably the trade unions. This is what Middlemas (1979) means by a continuous contract, in which the interests involved became governing institutions. It implied that the art of government was as much one of harmonizing the wishes of groups in civil society as of imposing a set of policies on them.

The second theme refers to a *range of policies* that were pursued by governments of both parties between the late 1940s and the mid-1970s. This range is often referred to by the names of its two alleged creators – William Beveridge and John Maynard Keynes. 'Beveredgeism' symbolized a commitment both to the collective provision of comprehensive welfare services in order to promote what was known as social citizenship, and to government involvement in the provision of other goods and services. Keynesianism meant government use of fiscal and monetary techniques to regulate the level of aggregate demand so as to create full employment. Welfare capitalism, or the mixed or managed economy, or Keynesian social democracy, are the terms most often used to describe the elements of the post-war consensus. A student of the 1951 Churchill Government, clearly a potential turning-point, claims that it 'cemented the post-war consensus which continued, though under increasing strain, until Margaret Thatcher's victory in May 1979' (Seldon, in Hennessy and Seldon, 1987, p. 81). According to Middlemas: 'The year 1945 . . . began a period of twenty years when nearly all the deep objectives of the state – in economic planning, social welfare, harmony and the avoidance of crises – seemed to have been achieved' (Middlemas, 1979, p. 371).

The Attlee Settlement

From the perspective of 1988 it seems clear that post-war British politics has been through two formative periods. The first covers the years 1945–51, the period of the first majority Labour Governments; the second covers the years of the Thatcher Governments. In the first period, as we have suggested, the main planks of what has been called the post-war political consensus were laid down. That period has been seen in the history books as representing the triumph of collectivist ideas and of the Labour Party and the working class identified with them. The planks were:

1 *the mixed economy*. The 1945 Labour manifesto advocated the public ownership of basic utilities and an active role for

government in managing the economy in pursuit of certain social and economic objectives. A number of industries and services were taken over by the state and much of the rest of the economy operated within guidelines laid down by the government. This more active role for the state grew out of the wartime experience. A mix of public and private ownership was largely accepted by governments until the late 1970s.

2 *full employment*. The commitment to run the economy at a level to provide full employment was accepted in the White Paper on Employment in 1944. In line with Keynesian ideas, governments accepted the duty of managing demand as a means of producing full employment. The policy succeeded. Compared to the double digit unemployment figures of the 1930s, the level did not exceed an average of 3 per cent in any full year between 1948 and 1970.

3 *conciliation of the trade unions*. Trade unions were accepted as an estate of the realm in wartime, not least because their cooperation was required for the war effort. After the war their bargaining position was helped by full employment and by the enhanced consultative status they were granted by Labour and then by succeeding Conservative governments.

4 *welfare*. The key date in the emergence of the modern welfare state was the Beveridge report of 1942 on *Social Insurance and Allied Services* (Command Paper 6404). This proposed that existing schemes of welfare support be consolidated to provide a universal national scheme. In 1945 and 1946 legislation provided for family allowances, sickness benefits and national assistance. In 1948 the National Health Service was established to provide treatment free, as of right.

5 *retreat from empire, Britain's role as a nuclear power and membership of the Atlantic Alliance*. At the end of the war Britain was the only imperial and West European state with the status of a world power. Between 1945 and 1951 the Labour Government began a process of disengagement from empire, starting with the grant of independence to India and Pakistan in 1947, and promoted the idea of the Commonwealth, an association of equal states. It also helped to create

the American-led Atlantic Alliance and started to develop an independent nuclear deterrent. Membership of European economic and political institutions was not at this time on the political agenda but became so in the 1960s. Questions of defence posture (particularly on the retention of nuclear weapons) and possible membership of the new European Community caused significant divisions in the Labour Party and, to a lesser degree, within the Conservatives. Yet these questions did not, apart from the period of Hugh Gaitskill's leadership of the Labour Party, cause difficulties for the leadership of either party.

These policy goals formed something of a social democratic package. It was a middle way, neither free market capitalist (as in the United States) nor state socialist (as it was to emerge in Eastern Europe). Success in the war had vindicated the active state and it was widely felt that the post-war reconstruction of society and economy should similarly be guided by the government. Succeeding Conservative governments accepted many of the policies, on the grounds that full employment and state welfare were electorally popular and that the cooperation of major interests like business and the trade unions was necessary to govern the country. Today, both New Right Conservatives and far-left socialists would complain that before 1979 social democracy prevailed, regardless of which party was in government.

It is fair to claim that many of the ruling ideas on which the consensus rested were elitist. Like the Fabians, Beveridge and Keynes were paternalistic and technocratic, believing in the rule of expertise and the importance of basing policy on evidence and research. Not surprisingly, both were essentially non-party men. In 1944 Keynes tried to reassure the economist Hayek about the dangers which planning and collectivism posed to individual liberty, by writing that it would be safe 'if those carrying it out are rightly oriented in their own minds and hearts to the moral issue'. Both Keynes and Beveridge took for granted the authority of government and 'the agency of a benevolent state serviced by a technocratic elite' (Skidelsky, 1977, p. 62): they certainly did not wish for an anti-authoritarian egalitarianism to replace the existing power system. The senior civil service was in general supportive of Keynesianism and the collective provision of welfare, since both attempted to impose bureaucratic rationality on the inefficiencies and injustices of the market.

There was also a certain interdependence in the package of policies. Full employment would ease the demands on the welfare budget and enhance the bargaining position of the unions; provision of welfare was a means of gaining trade union acceptance of wage restraint; state intervention in the economy was important as a means of regulating demand. The ideas of Keynes and Beveridge legitimized a large public sector, state spending, state provision of welfare and active government.

Many forces produced a convergence of policy between governments. Public opinion seemed attached to many planks of the consensus and politicians calculated that the electorate would punish parties that veered too sharply from them. There developed the idea of a 'middle ground', represented by the consensus, which the electorate wanted. The British tradition of making policy by consultation with interests meant that any party in government would have to accommodate the persistent claims from major interests like the City, business and the unions. The permanence of the senior civil service was another factor. A number of permanent secretaries in the 1960s and 1970s had served their apprenticeships in Whitehall in the war years or under the 1945 Labour Government. Their sense of what was 'practical', or what one serving civil servant called 'ongoing reality', was a force for continuity and convergence. Many departments had their own stock of conventional wisdom which they imparted to a succession of ministers, and their advice was often of a balanced 'on the one hand this, on the other hand that' nature. The abandonment or adoption of some policies (such as public spending cutbacks, devaluations of the pound, applications for entry to the Common Market) were forced by economic and financial constraints. External factors too encouraged the retreat from empire, regardless of political preference.

It is also worth noting that broadly similar policy packages emerged in the post-war period in other West European states.

The growth of scientific thought and expertise appeared to weaken the appeal and relevance of traditional ideologies of the Left and Right, ideologies which, in any case, had been discredited by the experience of Nazism and Stalinism. In Sweden, Norway, Denmark, the Netherlands, Austria and West Germany, governments regularly (and in some cases formally) consulted the major producer interests in formulating economic policy. France and Belgium came to terms with demands for independence from their colonies. Affluence softened social and class polarization and narrowed policy differences between the parties of the Left and the Right. Christian Democratic parties in Italy and Germany, and the Gaullist party in France in the 1960s, made appeals across social classes. Labour or Social Democratic parties, particularly in Britain, Scandinavia and Germany, played down policies of state ownership and emphasized their ability to satisfy consumer demands. 'Conservative Socialism' and the pursuit of economic growth were the dominant ideologies by the 1950s and 1960s. The role of government, measured in terms of public employment, taxation and state spending levels, grew in all West European states between 1950 and 1980. In spite of differing histories, cultures, party systems and forms of government, Western industrial states made increasing provision for welfare, and pursued full employment policies.

The Thatcher reaction

The second era of change has been that beginning in 1979, with the first of Mrs Thatcher's election victories. This period has seen the triumph of the Conservative Party, the rejection of much of the Attlee settlement, and the assertion by policy makers of a number of free market ideas – in a word, 'Thatcherism'. According to Peter Jenkins (1987) we are now living through a 'post-Socialist era'. The first three of the above planks have effectively been scrapped or eroded and the fourth, state provision of welfare, is increasingly being questioned. Government is no longer expected to own large parts of industry, to maintain full employment, or to negotiate its policies with trade unions. Mrs Thatcher was the first party leader to campaign on a platform of breaking with both aspects of the post-war consensus – policy style and particular policies. Her administrations have produced something of a revolution not only in British politics but also in the Conservative Party. She has frequently attacked the consensus and identified it with shabby compromises or ducking necessary 'tough' decisions. She knows, of course, that the term has become a code word used by those criticizing herself. But she also wishes to make her own ideas prevail; the collectivist, egalitarian values of 1945 should be replaced by those of individualism and freedom. In a prepared speech in the 1979 general election she compared herself to the 'Old Testament Prophets, who did not say "Brothers, I want a consensus. They said: This is my faith. This is what I passionately believe. If you believe it too, then come with me."' Political convictions and principles were, in her view, incompatible with consensus as a style of governing.

We argue that the most creative periods in post-war British politics can be associated with the Attlee and Thatcher administrations. These are the bookends, as it were, of modern British political history. In the space of a short book it is not possible to write a study of these two periods. Our purpose is rather:

1 to establish the nature of the post-war inter-party agreement and continuity in policies. While we accept that there was a post-war consensus and that it was widely talked about at the time, we are also aware of the limits of the agreement and continuity between governments;
2 to examine the nature of the breakdown of that continuity in the five policy areas listed above. The breakdown occurred largely from the mid-1970s onwards. Thatcherism might be regarded, not unfairly, as an attempt to impose a new policy framework or a new set of parameters to replace those of the old post-war consensus.

Did the consensus ever exist?

There is a problem about using the term consensus as a synonym for cross-party agreement. After all, disagreement about ends and means is the life blood of politics. Political disagreement arises inevitably from human diversity and the clash of individual and group interests. Politics is the activity of reconciling, in a fashion, these differences and establishing a common policy for society. An obvious problem follows: the idea of consensus is at odds with political activity. Was nothing at stake in general elections, were different party programmes false labels, was the party clash little more than a cover for rival personal ambitions? One has only to consider the bitter mood at the time of the Suez Canal conflict (1956), the resistance of trade unions and local authorities to Mr Heath during his free market period (1970–2), or the miners' strike which brought about the February 1974 election, for any idea of complete agreement to become wholly unrealistic. At the beginning of our period, the last eighteen months of the Attlee Government (1950–1) were marked by intense inter-party conflict in the House of Commons, and the plan to nationalize the steel industry was a cause of all-out political warfare that revealed stark differences in policy assumptions. Later, in the 1970s, S. E. Finer argued that the problem with Britain was that politics was insufficiently consensual and marked by frequent changes in policy.

It is possible to put forward the view that the consensus was nothing of the sort, that it is a myth. Indeed, Ben Pimlott (1988) has recently queried the assumption of near unanimity in post-war politics. He claims that politicians during the 1960s and early 1970s thought that they were divided on fundamental issues. Pimlott thinks that the idea of consensus is an artefact of historians and commentators who look back nostalgically to a pre-1979 era of alleged good feeling. They have been reinforced by New Right commentators who wish to discredit many pre-1979 ruling ideas and compromises and stress 1979 as a turning point, rather in the way that some historians in France argue that the return to power of de

Gaulle in 1958 saw the beginning of the post-war French recovery.

The record does not support Pimlott's doubts. Consider, for example, two areas, immigration and education, which are not discussed at length in this book. A good deal of rhetoric suggests that the Conservative and Labour Parties have differed fundamentally on these issues: Labour has been 'open door' on immigration, the Conservatives restrictive; and the Conservatives have been hostile to 'comprehensive schools', and Labour strongly supportive. In 1951, however (to look at immigration first), Labour nearly adopted controls on immigration from the New Commonwealth, as did the Conservatives in 1955. But at elite level there was agreement on not limiting such immigration. It was in response to back-bench concern over increasing immigration that the Conservatives then finally imposed limits on Commonwealth immigration in 1962. Although Labour bitterly opposed that measure, when it was in government it further tightened controls, in 1965 and 1968. More restrictions, other than those on EEC nationals seeking to enter the country for employment, have since been imposed by Conservative legislation in 1971 and 1980. For the last two decades elite agreement on immigration has been maintained by largely ignoring the issue; certainly party leaders have been reluctant to go public on it. It is worth noting that Enoch Powell's ministerial career was destroyed after he raised the issue in his 'rivers of blood' speech in 1968, and Mrs Thatcher, as opposition leader, embarrassed colleagues when she said in a television interview in 1978 that people felt 'swamped' by immigrants.

In the area of secondary education, the wartime Education Act (1944) inaugurated a tripartite system – grammar, secondary modern and technical schools. The 1945 Labour Government did not abolish private education or press ahead with comprehensive schools, as left-wingers wanted. The tripartite system dominated until 1964, when the Labour Government switched to support of comprehensives. Labour introduced an order in 1965 making comprehensive schooling mandatory, by insisting that all local authorities submit plans for reorganization. The new Conservative Government withdrew the order in 1970, leaving the decision about reorganization with the local authorities. Labour reimposed the order on its return to office in 1974, and the new Conservative government in 1979 withdrew it again. On the surface, policy has clearly been discontinuous, according to which party is in office. Yet by 1979 more than 90 per cent of secondary schools were comprehensive and over a period of more than 20 years the largest number of such schools was actually created under a Conservative minister of education, Margaret Thatcher (1970–4).

Pimlott also points to such features in the 1950s and 1960s as the high levels of party identification, class-based voting, trade union members' electoral support for Labour, and the stability of individual voting patterns. These are adduced as evidence of sharp differences between the parties. They are irrelevant, however, to the thesis of consensus – the continuity of policy between governments.

Marxist commentators have claimed that the so-called consensus exists but is little more than a particular form of the ideas of the ruling class, which represents the interest of capital. The dominant value system and its version of the national interest reconcile the mass of workers to inequalities and to the established political and economic order. The system is able to do so because of the corrupting effects of parliamentary politics on the political leadership of the working class. The Labour Party has never deviated from its belief in gradualist parliamentary methods and has never mounted a fundamental attack on the political system or economic order. For one critic, the history of the Labour Party since 1931 (when the Labour prime minister, Ramsay MacDonald, abandoned the Labour Government to lead a national coalition government) has been 'MacDonaldism without MacDonald' (Miliband 1961). Whenever the interests of capitalism and the values of socialism have been in conflict a Labour government has always supported the first. Its regular resort to incomes policies, protection of the pound, and the attempt in 1969 to impose sanctions upon the trade unions, are all in keeping with the policy of winning or maintaining the confidence of business and the holders of sterling. In other words, a Labour government, by accepting the political consensus which is advantageous to capitalism, denies its own values and the interests of the working class. More generally, Miliband (1969, p. 69) has said:

One of the most important aspects of the political life of advanced capitalism is precisely that the disagreements *between those political leaders who have genuinely been able to gain high office* have very seldom been the fundamental kind these leaders and other people so often suggest. What is really striking... is not their many differences but the extent of their agreement on truly fundamental issues. (Miliband's emphasis)

Thus the consensus becomes merely the ability of the elite to incorporate the leaders of those whom it exploits.

Our view is that 'consensus' is not helpful if it is understood to mean absence of disagreement or simply elite collusion. It is more appropriate to think of it as *a set of parameters which bounded the set of policy options regarded by senior politicians and civil servants as administratively practicable, economically affordable and politically acceptable*. In other words, the disagreements between the party elites were contained. In the late nineteenth century the constitutional lawyer A. V. Dicey said that the Conservative and Liberal Parties divided on differences which are 'important but not fundamental'. Addison has this in mind when he talks of a post-war settlement on policy. On welfare, for example, it was a question of the level of benefits and range of entitlements; on the retreat from empire, a question of pace and timing; on public ownership, a question of the extent of state regulation. No Labour government seriously entertained ideas of widespread public ownership and no Conservative one until 1979 had tried to dismantle the nationalized sector.

Of course there were party differences of rhetoric (particularly in Parliament, at annual party conferences and during general elections) and of emphasis (Conservatives, for example, were keener than Labour to cut income tax, Labour more sympathetic than Conservatives to local authority housing). The Tory discourse was predominantly one of freedom of opportunity, preserving Britain's influence in the world, encouraging and rewarding enterprise and fostering a property-owning democracy. Labour's language emphasized equality, economic planning, fairness, advancing the interests of working people and their families, and the multiracial Commonwealth.

In addition, both the Labour and Conservative Parties contained wings which dissented from the ruling orthodoxy. In opposition, these voices grew stronger in the councils of each party. Some Conservatives called for more individualistic and free market policies, lower direct taxation and reduced state spending. They opposed the retreat from empire and were critical of the country's obviously subordinate relationship with the United States. The Labour Left advocated unilateral nuclear disarmament, major extensions to public ownership and a harsher climate for private business and wealth. If one listened exclusively to these voices then the parties appeared to be far apart. The *governmentalists* in both political parties, however, were overwhelmingly drawn from the centre of the political spectrum and, for all the differences of nuance and rhetoric, it is the continuity of policy which stands out. Thus consensus politics are inextricably linked with policy-making as an elite process (carried out by senior ministers, civil servants, producer interest groups and communicators) and with the existence of a government that possesses authority. It is worth noting, though, that among the population there was much support for policies which the elite had not supported. This was the case, for example, with restricting immigration during the 1960s and early 1970s (as Enoch Powell was to demonstrate), restoring capital punishment and not entering the European Community. Moreover, the inter-party agreement on goals (maintaining, for example, full employment, or the mixed economy) was stronger than on policy means.

Origins

The date of the origins of the themes that would form the substance of the consensus is the subject of disagreement among historians. In so far as government formally acknowledged the power of major economic interests and the need to bargain with them, *the 1914—18 war* was significant. Trade unions achieved great influence because government needed workers to meet production targets and men for troops. Keith Middlemas, in his important *The Politics of Industrial Society*, dates the emergence of a close relationship between producer interests and governments from this period.

It is also possible to see many of the post-war programmes emerging from *the inter-war years*. Some of the policies built incrementally on earlier policies. This is true of the National Health Service, Beveridge's reform of welfare, and the public corporation form of nationalization which built on Herbert Morrison's model of the London Passenger Transport Board. Policy was in large measure a form of learning and adaptation, attempts to find solutions to immediate problems. By the early 1920s the two major parties were Conservative and Labour. These were able to adjust to an era of what has been called *collectivist* politics; a mass electorate, active government and influential producer groups. Conservatives could adapt because historically they believed in the authority of government and perceived society not as a collection of individuals or classes but as an organic unity. Labour could adapt because the working class wanted jobs, housing and welfare and looked to the state to help provide them. The casualty of the new politics was the Liberal Party, whose individualistic view of society and traditional hostility to state-led collectivism shackled it with an outdatedness that the New Liberalism of the early twentieth century had not been able to eradicate.

Although the government's economic policy in the 1930s was pre-Keynesian, ministers nevertheless adopted some measures to combat unemployment and pursued a regional policy to encourage firms to locate in the more economically depressed parts of the United Kingdom. The state had already begun to manage particular enterprises; for example, the London Passenger Transport Authority, the British Broadcasting Corporation and the Central Electricity Generating Board were all run as public corporations and provided models for later nationalized industries. State welfare provision, compared to that of many other Western states, was generous. In these years a middle opinion developed, across the political parties, that capitalism must – and could – be reformed. Ideas about the mixed economy, promoting employment and the welfare state were advancing. The government, however, refused to accept the validity of the ideas put forward by this middle opinion and was reluctant to strengthen the consultation rights of a trade union movement whose strength had in any case been damaged by the 1926 General Strike and by high unemployment.

The ideas and some of the practices of consensus existed before the Second World War. The importance of the war was that it created circumstances in which discrete ideas merged into a more or less coherent package and public expectations about the role of government changed. Thus a third interpretation stresses the formative role of *the wartime (1940—5) Coalition Government*, as it faced the pressure to mobilize society for total war.

Increasingly, politicians adopted a cross-party approach to tackling problems and the experience of working together helped to educate many in the merits of the other side. Addison points out that by inviting the Labour and Liberal Parties to join the coalition, Churchill broke the Conservative political hegemony of the inter-war years. Addison also claims that there was a major shift in public opinion between 1940 and 1942. Policy makers and ordinary men and women accepted that there should be an active role for the state in social and economic management, and thought that something should be done after the war to improve the quality of life for ordinary people. In wartime the trade unions were represented on a wide range of government committees. The appointment of Ernest Bevin, General Secretary of the Transport and General Workers' Union, as minister of labour in 1940 was a symbol and guarantee of labour's influence. In 1943 the government, under pressure from the House of Commons, accepted the Beveridge proposals for social security.

Since Churchill devoted his energies to the war, Labour ministers had more opportunity to shape the domestic agenda. A Cabinet Committee on Reconstruction, established in 1943, reached broad agreement on social security, education, family or child allowances, greater state intervention in industry (though not nationalization) and Keynesian budgeting techniques. The Coalition Government produced the 1944 Employment White Paper, passed the Education Act (1944) and the Family Allowances Act (1945), and made some progress on the Beveridge proposals for social insurance. Late in the war Attlee replied to a Labour critic that he felt that there had been a significant shift in opinion during the war about the need for planning and full employment; in discussions with colleagues of other parties he had found 'on many matters more agreement than you would expect' and noted that there were 'limits to the extent to which the clock can be put forward or back' (Pelling, 1970, p. 308).

A fourth key period is *the early years of the 1951 Churchill Government*. A crucial proof of policy agreement is when the opposition assumes office and then carries on with the broad policy framework of the outgoing government. In the 1951 election campaign Labour warned voters that a Conservative government would cut back the social services, provoke the trade unions, endanger full employment and pursue very different and more aggressive foreign and colonial policies. The major study of the government laconically notes 'in fact none of these prophesies was fulfilled' (Seldon, 1981, p. 421). On nationalization, the Conservative opposition had bitterly contested only the case of iron and steel. They did not oppose the 1946 National Insurance Act on second and third readings, although Labour's plans for the health service did arouse strong opposition. In many areas, Conservatives claimed that the Labour Government was simply following lines already laid down by the wartime coalition.

Churchill told his joint principal private secretary that his priorities were 'houses and meat, and not being scuppered'. Only two of the nationalized industries were denationalized, the welfare state was largely untouched and the thrust of foreign and colonial policy was unchanged. If many of the senior civil servants serving the 1945 Labour Government had also served the wartime coalition, so the Conservatives inherited some powerful men from Labour; Seldon (1981, p. 7) points in particular to the roles of Sir Edward Bridges, the head of the civil service (1945–56), and of Sir Norman Brook, secretary of the Cabinet (1947–62).

Consensus and decline

Politicians, whether consciously or not, derive lessons from the recent past and have a vested interest in encouraging the acceptance of their particular interpretation of it. Activists on the political Left and Right have condemned the consensus for policy failures and Britain's economic decline, while so-called moderates have contrasted it favourably with the record of Mrs Thatcher. What has given this debate its intensity is the widespread belief that the consensus not only coincided with but actually caused a long period of national decline.

It is important, therefore, that we try to make sense of *this period*, because of its powerful influence on the period in which we now live. Most inhabitants of Britain between the ages of 20 and 60 have lived through either or both of the Attlee and Thatcher years, and almost all of the politically influential figures – in the political parties, senior civil service, finance, business, trade unions and the mass media – are products of these years.

The large literature on Britain's decline concentrates mainly on the relative economic decline and the loss of 'great power' status. Some explanations are narrowly economic and point to specific mistaken policies and decisions, such as excessive public spending, Keynesianism, failure to devalue before 1967, Luddite trade unions, putting the needs of finance ahead of those of industry, and so on. Some are historical and cultural, dealing with the ideas and values of the elites and the public. Others are more explicitly political and point to the need for constitutional reform. One example of the latter in the 1970s was the critique of the two-party system offered by the *adversary politics* school (Finer, 1975). This argued that the parties had become more polarized and that changes of government were producing sharp, frequent and damaging reversals of policy. Moreover, a party with 40 per cent or less of the popular vote could form a government with a clear majority of seats in the Commons. If Britain adopted a more proportional electoral system, a party would have to gain nearly 50 per cent of the vote or enter a coalition to form a government. Electoral reform might actually produce more consensual and continuous policies.

In so far as the post-war consensus was associated with policies of high public spending and high taxes, state intervention in the economy and the pursuit of egalitarianism, it has been a target for radical Conservatives. Mrs Thatcher and her supporters have identified such policies with Britain's decline. Sir Keith Joseph in 1979 attacked six post-war 'poisons . . . which wreck a country's prosperity and full employment; excessive government spending, high direct taxation, egalitarianism, excessive nationalisation, a politicised trade union movement associated with Luddism, and an anti-enterprise culture (other countries had one or two) . . . we're the only country that has all six' (cited in Heald, 1983, p. 7). The identification of the consensus with collectivism, interventionism and egalitarianism thus lies at the heart of the Right's hostility to it. In wanting to break with so much of the post-war period, Mrs Thatcher and Sir Keith have by implication also been blaming some of their Conservative predecessors. Such an attitude has led Sir Ian Gilmour to write that Conservatives will, 'soon have to choose their heroes from a shortlist of Montagu Norman, Lord Eldon, Judge Jeffreys and Herbert Hoover' (1983, p. 96).

A sustained onslaught on the wartime government has recently been offered by Correlli Barnett, in *The Audit of War* (1986). This is a study of how Britain's industrial society coped with war. Significantly, the argument of the book appears to have influenced a number of Conservative leaders, including Sir Keith Joseph. Drawing on a number of wartime government reports, Barnett shows how bad Britain's performance was in the aircraft, shipbuilding, machine tool and motor vehicle industries, among others. Barnett blames the poor quality of management and education and the neglect of wealth creation. In particular he blames the wartime coalition and the post-war Labour Government for wrongly concentrating on social welfare rather than on capital investment and training of the labour force. Britain was beguiled, Barnett argues, by promises of a new Jerusalem, represented by the welfare state, better housing and full employment. Indeed, reading the book, one wonders how Britain actually won the war.

The political Left regards the post-war consensus with mixed feelings. Some have regarded the Attlee Government as the high point of parliamentary socialism. Using a disciplined Parliamentary majority the government implemented a radical programme and produced a peaceful revolution. Yet critics on the Left have also regarded the 1945 Government as an example of the party's coming to terms with capitalism and missing the opportunity for a radical redistribution of social and economic power. Nationalization, for example, involved generous compensation to shareholders, management by an impersonal bureaucracy and no moves towards worker control. Industry remained largely in private hands and egalitarian changes were marginal. Private health and education continued and Britain was locked into a subordinate position to the US in international, military and economic affairs. The ambiguity with which the Left regards the Attlee achievement can be seen in the contrasting assessments of it made by Tony Benn. He has described it as a model which succeeding Labour Governments have failed to emulate; but he has also, more recently, denounced it for its statist methods and hostility to working class control.

What, therefore, was to be done? The 1979 Tory leadership claimed that the application of new policies (monetarism, enterprise economy and limited government) and the assertion of political will were the answer. There would be no more U-turns and government would assert its democratically won authority against sectional interests. The Labour Left also called for stronger political will and more left-wing policies (more public ownership, economic planning, withdrawal from the European Community and greater public spending). The changes in the party's constitution after 1979 would make the parliamentary leadership more responsive to the activists.

Thus many influential people in both parties were at one in their desire to bury the post-war settlement. Non-party commentators pointed to another weakness of the consensus. It narrowed the range of policy options among the elites and excluded a number of desirable policies, such as privatisation, an end to rent control, entry into the EEC in the 1950s, the need to broaden the tax base and perhaps even a different policy for Northern Ireland. Gamble and Walkland (1984) are particularly persuasive critics of this.

Indeed, a recurring theme in a number of contemporary analyses was the weakness of government, even when supported by a stable parliamentary majority. Brian Chapman (*British Government Observed*, 1963) and Andrew Shonfield (*Modern Capitalism*, 1965) were early examples of this form of critique. In the 1970s pessimism about Britain's continuing economic weakness and apparently declining social cohesiveness deepened. Was Britain governable? Commentators observed the overweening ability of interest groups to veto changes which they found objectionable, notably incomes policies and early attempts to reform industrial relations. Samuel Beer, in *Britain Against Itself* (1982) talked of pluralistic stagnation, the stalemate in public policy that arose from the ability of interest groups to frustrate policy initiatives. Correlli Barnett complains of the failure of Britain to become, like France and Japan, a *dirigiste* state leading industry to promote higher economic growth. David Marquand (1988a) has similarly complained of the failure of Britain to evolve as a developmental state, which directs market forces.

Much criticism of the consensus, however, is overdone and sometimes lacks historical perspective. Critics of Barnett observe that Britain's relative industrial decline has gone on for a century or more (though the war years may still have been a missed opportunity) and that many other Western states achieved a more impressive economic recovery than Britain in spite of high levels of welfare provision. Moreover, in countries like Japan, Italy and France state intervention in the economy was at least as great as in Britain. Defenders of the consensus may also point to the steady improvement in living standards, low unemployment and inflation, social unity and political stability for the first 30 post-war years. Although in the early 1980s Beer was profoundly pessimistic about what he saw as the pluralistic stagnation in British politics, only a few years earlier he had admiringly commented: 'Happy the country in which consensus and conflict are ordered in a dialectic that makes of the political arena at once a market of interests and a forum for debate of fundamental moral consensus' (1969, p. 390).

It is, however, difficult to deny that, particularly during the 1970s, the familiar policies were ceasing to produce the desired outputs. On economic league tables Britain continued to perform poorly. In the 1970s inflation averaged 11 per cent annually and economic growth less than 2 per cent; the International Monetary Fund (IMF) had to intervene in 1976 to support the pound; recalcitrant trade unions indirectly precipitated the collapse of the Heath Government in 1974 and the Callaghan Government in 1979. Incomes policies, a central plank in the economic policy of both governments, had been challenged and destroyed by the unions; their fate demonstrated the weakness of government.

Political generations often react against their immediate predecessors. Just as 1945 meant a rejection of the inter-war period, so 1979 inaugurated a period in which the post-war consensus came to be held up as an anti-model by politicians in both parties. It is impossible as of now to say whether Mrs Thatcher's Government has reversed national decline or whether the post-war consensus caused that decline. Indeed, the very concept of national decline is so impregnated with value judgements that it needs, particularly in the short period we are dealing with, to be handled with care. What can be said is that there are continuities in government policy and governing style between 1945 and the 1970s that make the idea of consensus a useful explanatory device. Whether the consensus was beneficial to British society as a whole is a different type of question and one that it is probably too early to answer.

2 The Mixed Economy

Before 1914 the framework of the capitalist system was accepted by both major parties. This did not mean that government absented itself from the market-place – as a minister in the 1906 Liberal Government, for example, Winston Churchill organized the purchase of what would become British Petroleum – but it did mean that the idea of widespread public ownership of industry or financial institutions was rejected. Between the wars, however, the emergence of the Labour Party as the main opposition to the Conservatives ensured that public ownership became one of the principal items on the political agenda, a position that it has never since lost. In Clause IV of its 1918 programme, the Labour Party pledged itself to public ownership, or 'common ownership of the means of production, distribution and exchange and the best obtainable system of popular administration and control of each industry or service'. The party defended this policy in terms of promoting efficiency (economic planning would end the chaos of capitalist production), social justice (redistribution), industrial democracy (popular control) and, perhaps above all, fellowship. The political circumstances of the time, however, gave Labour few opportunities to implement their vision and it was, in fact, the Conservatives who were responsible for such interventionism as there was. The 1924–9 Conservative Government placed the BBC and electricity supply under public corporations and practised what some historians have called 'Tory socialism'. In the 1930s the Conservative-dominated National Government assisted in the reorganization of declining industries, to protect them from overseas competition.

Public ownership and party politics

The major extension of state control and increased economic intervention during the Second World War significantly advanced the case for public ownership. Thus by 1945 there were pragmatic as well as ideological reasons for state ownership of those industries or services which were basic utilities, monopolies, or of strategic importance. The wartime Coalition Government had already issued reports concerning the future organization of the Bank of England and the coal, electricity and gas industries. Each clearly envisaged a greater role for the state and there was a general recognition of the need for reorganization and increased investment in many of these industries, particularly coal and railways. Labour's 1945 election manifesto promised to transfer into public ownership coal, rail transport, civil aviation, road passenger and freight transport, and the electricity, gas, and iron and steel industries. This programme was carried out as follows:

Nationalization Statutes
1946	Bank of England Act
1946	Coal Industry Nationalization Act
1946	Civil Aviation Act
1947	Electricity Act
1947	Transport Act
1948	Gas Act
1949	Iron and Steel Act

Some of these industries, notably coal and rail, had poor records of economic return or industrial relations, while others, such as gas and electricity, had better histories. As the party of private enterprise the Conservatives were opposed to nationalization, yet they did not believe in the unregulated operation of the free market. As Sir Anthony Eden (Conservative prime minister 1955–7) once said, his was 'not the party of unbridled, brutal capitalism'. In the *Industrial Charter* (1947) the Party came to terms with full employment and the welfare state. But nationalization was different; this was a fundamental divide between the parties. Halting or reversing nationalization was associated with the Conservative Party's aims of defending individual freedom and enterprise. The 1951 manifesto promised to defend the British way of life, threatened by 'a Socialist state monopolising production, distribution and exchange [which] would be fatal to individual freedom'. The nationalization of iron and steel and road haulage aroused passionate Conservative opposition and the pledge of their return to the private sector.

The newly nationalized industries were run by public corporations, with the chairman and board members appointed by the sponsoring ministry. The boards were left largely free to run the industries but were instructed to 'break even' financially, taking one year with another. They had to combine social responsibility (for example, running trains on uneconomic routes) with commercial considerations.

In fact, the compromise between providing a public service and operating commercially did not work out satisfactorily. Ministers were empowered to give the boards directives of a general character but interfered in management prerogatives – such as pricing, employment, investment and location of sites – usually for political reasons. Public corporations, in contrast to private businesses, may borrow from the Treasury as well as the market. The declining rail, steel and coal industries all ran at a loss for many years and relied on Treasury subsidies. Over time, governments pressed for reductions in costs, greater return on capital and the meeting of financial targets.

The Tories and the mixed economy

The public ownership measures were largely accepted, however unwillingly, by the Conservative governments after 1951 (King, 1973, p. 307; Hogg, 1947). The Churchill administration denationalized only iron and steel (1953) and road haulage (1954) but for the rest it did not wish to disrupt the industries. The consensual mood was expressed by Churchill when he said in 1951 that the nation needed 'several administrations, if only to allow for Socialist legislation to reach its full fruition'.

By 1951 some 20 per cent of industry and commerce was in the hands of the state and the remainder, though privately owned, was subject to a variety of government rules and regulations. Government policies for regional and economic development, tariffs, taxation, contracts (for example, in defence or shipbuilding) and, in the 1960s and 1970s, prices and incomes controls, increased this influence. By 1963 Harold Macmillan had converted his party to indicative economic planning and sought to persuade the trade unions of the need for incomes policies. Indicative planning did not involve a central plan but was designed to improve coordination between different sectors of the economy. Macmillan also established the National Economic Development Council in 1962 as a forum in which government, the unions and employers could consider ways of promoting faster economic growth. There was no visible interest from government in reducing the size of the public sector.

In opposition between 1966 and 1970, the Conservatives became more sympathetic to free market solutions. Indeed, the 1970 Heath Government started out with such policies (in a famous phrase, a minister promised not to rescue 'lame duck' firms). In the first two years it sought to disengage from the economy, taxes and public spending were cut, and the previous Labour Government's Prices and Incomes Board and Industrial Reorganization Corporation were abolished. But by 1972 the Heath Government embraced far-reaching statutory controls over prices and incomes, and actually extended public ownership to the economically vulnerable Rolls-Royce and Upper Clyde Shipyard as a means of saving jobs. In the interest of stability it accepted the status of the steel industry, which Labour had renationalized in 1968. The Industry Act (1972) empowered the government to intervene on a large scale in firms. For various pragmatic reasons Conservative governments accepted and were prepared to consolidate public ownership. Attempts to 'roll back the state' had failed. In spite of the adversarial rhetoric, broad agreement about the existing boundaries between the public and private sectors continued to be a significant element in the post-war consensus.

Labour and the 'commanding heights'

Meanwhile the Labour Party had been rethinking the role of public ownership. It is worth remembering that a number of Labour leaders had always been reluctant nationalizers. It was pressure from the floor rather than initiative at the top which committed the party to the ambitious programme approved at the 1944 party conference. The emphasis was firmly on nationalization as a means of improving economic efficiency rather than promoting industrial democracy. Although there was a shopping list of industries for nationalization in the 1950 manifesto, the narrowness of the party's election victory strengthened the hands of consolidators like Morrison for the 1951 election. In 1959, apart from promising to renationalize iron and steel and road haulage, the manifesto threatened to take over only industries or firms which were shown to be 'failing the nation'.

Anthony Crosland's influential book, *The Future of Socialism* (1956), became a Bible for the so-called revisionists in the Labour Party who wished to revise party attitudes towards public ownership. It argued that capitalism had been reformed and was now serving the nation well. Governments had various instruments such as the budget, investment and controls on the location of industry to influence the large corporations. Keynesian demand management could even out the cycles of boom and slump and deliver full employment. Public ownership, therefore, was no longer so important: management rather than ownership was decisive. Crosland argued that the new goal of socialism should be equality, which could be advanced through greater public spending and narrowing the differences in wealth and income.

After Labour's third successive election defeat in 1959, the party leader, Hugh Gaitskell, tried to get the party to rewrite Clause IV of the party constitution. He argued that the clause's open-ended commitment to public ownership laid the party open to damaging charges that it wished to nationalize everything. The party, however, refused to agree to a watering down of what was a fundamental part of its value system. Yet apart from the renationalization of iron and steel, the 1964 Labour Government did little. Symbolically the party remained wedded to public ownership but in practice the revisionists had won.

But the victory proved to be a temporary one. The debate over public ownership became a fundamental divide between Labour's left and right wings. Whilst revisionists were prepared to make greater use of the market, public ownership remained the litmus test of socialism for the party's Left. For the latter, Clause IV made Labour distinctive and was essential if the party was serious about economic planning, curbing market forces and moving from a capitalist to a socialist society. Unless the government could control what Aneurin Bevan had termed 'the commanding heights of the economy', it would not be able to deliver other radical measures.

After its 1970 election defeat the Labour Party moved to the left. An assault on Crosland's *The Future of Socialism* was presented by Stuart Holland's *The Challenge of Socialism* (1975). He argued that the rise of multinational corporations meant that the mixed economy and Keynesian techniques of demand management no longer worked; managers of the multinationals could always escape national controls and undermine government policies on employment, price and investment. Hence 'without public ownership and control of the dominant means of production, distribution and exchange, the state will never manage the strategic features of the economy in the public interest' (Holland, 1975, p. 15). In *Labour's Programme 1973*, the party declared its intention to take over the leading financial institutions and 25 major companies. In government from 1974, the leadership was more cautious. It took into public ownership only the aerospace and shipbuilding industries, both of which were ailing and already in receipt of substantial state aid. In 1975 it also established a National Enterprise Board (NEB), with powers to make voluntary planning agreements with firms and extend public ownership. Yet the Labour Governments of 1974–9 did not substantially extend the mixed economy. The NEB did little beyond rescuing financially troubled firms like British Leyland and Chrysler. A persistent economic crisis, a minority government, and, not least, the reluctance of senior ministers to engage in what they saw as ideological adventurism, ensured that the public/private sector boundary remained largely intact. This caution was unsatisfactory to the Left of the party, which increasingly regarded the growing economic crisis, notably the decline of corporate profits and rising unemployment, as a failure of British capitalism. The Left welcomed the crisis as an opportunity for the state to take over profitable and strategic-ally important sectors of the economy. It rallied around the so-called Alternative Economic Strategy, which called for massive state ownership, import controls (to protect industry and firms vulnerable to foreign competition) and withdrawal from the EEC. It was a programme for socialism in one country.

By the late 1970s, the mixed economy consensus had few friends and was widely regarded as a failure. While the influential left wing of the Labour party wanted much more nationalization, the Conservative Party under Mrs Thatcher was committed to more free market policies. Nationalization, however, is one of those areas of the post-war consensus where practice and rhetoric have differed most widely. With the exception of its application to the iron and steel industry the continuity of this policy was the most notable feature of the whole period. At the level of belief and self-identification, nationalization separated the parties in a fundamental way; it provided justification for the belief that democratic politics is about choice. But it also showed, in substance, how limited and shadowy that choice was.

Privatization

By 1979 the state-owned industrial sector accounted for 10 per cent of GDP, 15 per cent of national investment and 7 per cent of employment. Some of the publicly owned industries had bad industrial relations records and poor productivity, notably British Rail, British Leyland, British Steel and British Coal

(Pryke, 1981), and surveys suggested that proposals for further nationalization were a vote loser for Labour. Indeed, in the 1979 'Winter of Discontent' the greatest inconvenience was caused in the public services. Rather than potential profits being used to benefit the consumer (as envisaged in 1918), the absence of the profit incentive seemed to lead both to inefficiencies and to producer sovereignty, and the huge losses incurred by some industries imposed a burden on the taxpayer. On the other hand, the post-war period also seemed to suggest that attempts to roll back state involvement in industry were doomed to failure. However unpopular, the mixed economy seemed a permanent feature of British life.

Opposition to public ownership had existed for a number of years on the free market wing of the Conservative Party. In the 1970s its influence grew, as problems of inflation, public spending pressures, union power and overstaffing all focused on the nationalized industries. Under Mrs Thatcher the 1979 Conservative Government was more convinced than its predecessors of the merits of a market-orientated economy. The Government originally set itself modest goals – to restore to the private sector the recently nationalized shipbuilding and aerospace companies, review the activities of the British National Oil Corporation, sell off state shares in the National Freight Corporation and National Enterprise Board and relax the licensing system of bus companies. Essentially, the programme sought to recreate the balance prevailing in 1970 and could not be seen as a major breach with the consensus. Conservatives had traditionally wanted to make nationalized industries more efficient and accountable. There was nothing to anticipate the scale of privatization that was to follow. Moreover, sceptics remembered that Mr Heath's 1970 Government had started out with similar intentions but ended by actually extending state intervention.

Advocates of privatization in the Conservative Party pointed to a number of advantages. (W. H. Greenleaf (1987) notes that the term 'denationalization' dates back to the 1920s, the term 'privatization' to the 1950s.) They objected to the monopolistic and low risk position of many of the publicly owned industries and services; these too often responded, it was claimed, to political rather than consumer preferences and pre-empted investment funds from more productive parts of the economy. Critics added that the absence of commercial disciplines or of the threat of bankruptcy removed a stimulus to efficiency. In support they could point to the poor performance of many nationalized industries, particularly the low pre-tax real rates of return on capital. Finally, wage bargaining in much of the public sector had become more politicized and produced frequent confrontations with the central government, regardless of whether or not it had a statutory prices and incomes policy. In the 1970s public corporations had worse records on strikes than private corporations (Heald, 1983, p. 213). The classic confrontations of the Heath Government in 1974 and of the Callaghan Government in 1978–9 had largely been with workers in the public sector.

Privatization has essentially involved *either* the sale of state owned shares and assets to the workforce or to investors, *or* transferring the functions of public bodies to the private sector. Most forms of privatization have involved sales to the public. The early sales (often at subsantially discounted prices) proved popular with share buyers. The revenues raised by the sales were also useful in funding tax cuts and maintaining public spending levels. The two-stage sale of British Telecom raised nearly £4 billion, for the Exchequer, and that of British Gas £5 billion.

The programme has so far included the nation's telephone system, gas, the largest airline and airports. Water, electricity and steel are scheduled for privatization in the current (1987) Parliament. Parts of the coal and rail industries are likely candidates for privatization in the future. Some 600,000 jobs and a third of the state-owned industrial sector have so far been transferred and share ownership has expanded, from 7 per cent of the adult population in 1979 to 20 per cent in 1987. An added advantage for the government is that it has found itself freed from often difficult wage negotiations with powerful trade unions in the once nationalized industries.

The role of the market has also been enhanced by deregulation and by enabling private firms to compete in parts of the public sector. The state monopoly of express delivery services has been ended and controls over licensing and fares on long-distance coaching have been eased. The monopolies of solicitors over conveyancing and of opticians over prescribing spectacles have been abolished. The Housing Act of 1980, which gave council tenants with three years residence the right to buy their properties at a discount, has produced a massive increase in private home ownership. By 1988 over 1.2 million council properties had been transferred to private ownership. Some local authorities have put out to tender such services as refuse collection and hospital catering and laundry services. In 1988 the government confirmed its determination to carry on with this policy, by announcing that sports facilities run by local authorities would also be put out to private tender.

Supporters of the government point to the economic and, they claim, political freedoms which this programme has produced. They also stress that it has enhanced the authority of managers to manage and to make commercially sound decisions. Previous Conservative governments had largely accepted state ownership in the interest of policy continuity. But now, by rolling back state ownership, Mrs Thatcher has reversed the socialist ratchet. Critics, however, point to the failures in some areas to increase competition (for example, the Royal Ordnance Factory in 1988), and complain that some assets may have been sold off too cheaply. British Telecom and British Gas were sold as single units and enjoy monopoly or near-monopoly positions. Moreover, the revenues raised now have to be set against the profits forgone in future years. The Earl of Stockton (formerly Harold Macmillan), referred in a famous speech in the House of Lords in December 1984 to the programme as 'selling off the family silver'.

The inter-party agreement on public ownership until 1979 owed more to inertia than positive enthusiasm. Few front-benchers or civil servants thought large-scale privatization could be carried out and there was widespread fear that such an operation would provoke serious opposition from the unions and Labour Party. In fact the support was 'soft'; Conservative ministers were surprised at how easily the privatization measures were carried through, and the programme gathered momentum after 1983. Nationalization's natural supporters –

Labour and the unions – were much weaker after 1979, and in many cases the workforce and consumer were only too willing to buy shares in the privatized concerns.

Conclusion

Conservative ministers regard privatization as one of their outstanding successes and aim to extend the programme in the future. In conjunction with the privatization of local government programmes (in housing, refuse collection and education), this has clearly been a major exercise in denationalization. Labour at present resists further privatization and has promised to return British Gas and British Telecom to the public sector by means of what it terms 'social ownership'.

Meanwhile the Thatcher message of privatization has found echoes outside Britain and one can even talk of an international appreciation of its merits. In France the Chirac government of 1986–8 began to denationalize the companies taken over by the Socialists in the early 1980s. In Austria the new Socialist–Conservative coalition is turning to part-privatization of state-owned industries. In West Germany the Kohl government is also committed to a programme of privatization. In the United States, under President Reagan, a policy of deregulation and withdrawal of many government economic controls has also been carried through. Yet in none of these countries has the rolling back of state enterprise gone as far as in Britain. Privatization has been perhaps the most dramatic break with the post-war consensus in Britain. It symbolizes the government's rejection of the economic structures established after 1945 and its commitment to a free market philosophy that had fallen into widespread disrepute in the period when the consensus was established.

The privatization programme has caused severe difficulties for the Labour Party. Its ideological and emotional commitment to public ownership, its close links with public sector unions, and the leftwards shift in its policies after 1979 meant that it was bound to oppose privatization. Labour's 1983 election manifesto pledged an end to council house sales and promised to renationalize all the services which had been privatized by the Conservatives. Yet it was abundantly clear that the party suffered from its rejection of privatization. By 1987 Labour accepted council house sales and, although it has promised to take back British Gas and British Telecom into 'social ownership', it has also declared that renationalization will not be a priority for a future Labour Government. Instead, according to Neil Kinnock at the party's 1988 conference, Labour's aim should be to manage a market economy better than the Conservatives.

3 Full Employment

The policy goal of full employment is a good example of how the politicians of one generation so often tackle the major problems of their predecessors. Mass unemployment was the dominant economic and social feature of inter-war Britain; from 1940 it virtually disappeared for the next three decades. Yet in the inter-war years it seemed that nothing could be done about the scourge of large-scale unemployment. The concern of policy makers at the end of the First World War had been to bring about the restoration, as far as possible, of the pre-war policies. The pursuit of 'normalcy' (in the memorable phrase of US President Harding) meant that policy-makers rapidly abandoned the wartime controls on the economy, seeking instead to balance the budget, restrain public spending and rebuild the pre-war international financial and trading system. In fact Britain had permanently lost a number of overseas markets and its major export industries in textiles, coal, iron and steel and shipbuilding began a long decline.

Keynes and full employment

The economist John Maynard Keynes in the late 1920s was already working towards his theory that unemployment was caused by a deficiency of demand. Keynes heavily influenced the Liberal manifesto for the 1929 election, *We Can Conquer Unemployment*, which promised to cut unemployment by 500,000 through a Keynesian programme of deficit financing and public works. But the Liberals failed to make an electoral breakthrough and Treasury orthodoxy ruled the economic policies of both Conservative and (more surprisingly) Labour governments in the inter-war period. An alternative model, the USSR, showed that through state planning of the economy full employment could be achieved. But this could only be done at the cost of abandoning capitalism and political freedom. During the 1930s national unemployment figures were usually over 10 per cent and in most of Scotland, Wales and the north of England they were much higher. In this decade there developed a cross-party body of opinion that looked to the government to play a more active role in promoting economic expansion and employment.

During the war unemployment virtually disappeared as the economy worked at full capacity. The conscious pursuit of full employment as a goal of economic policy was then expressed in the 1944 White Paper on Employment (Command Paper 6527). In its opening words the government accepted 'as one of the primary aims and responsibilities the maintenance of a high and stable level of employment after the war'. In the 1945 general election, and for many general elections afterwards, all major political parties accepted the commitment to full employment. All parties claimed to be Keynesians but Labour alone declared its willingness to implement far-reaching controls over the private sector in pursuit of full employment. In the 1950s Labour regularly boasted that full employment was one of its greatest achievements while the Conservatives, determined to live down their reputation as the party of unemployment in the 1930s, pledged to maintain it.

Politicians calculated that maintaining full employment was good politics – it was essential if they were to win elections. Full employment was also good economics. In his report (see p. 73) Beveridge argued that full employment was essential if the welfare state was not to be swamped by excessive demands. He also pointed to the human benefits of being engaged in productive employment; paying unemployment benefit was 'inadequate [as] a provision for human happiness'.

Keynes was the genius who managed to reconcile state intervention in the economy with political freedom. The inter-war economic depression had shown that the economics of the market were not working as suggested by classical theory. This held that supply and demand would balance to provide full employment; supply created its own demand. If there was unemployment then it was because wages were too high. The requirements of the 'old' economics were a balanced budget and restraint in public spending. According to Winston Churchill, in his 1929 Budget speech, 'It is the orthodox Treasury dogma, steadfastly held, that whatever might be the political or social advantages, very little additional employment and no real permanent additional employment can in fact, as a general rule, be created by state borrowing and state expenditure.'

Yet Keynes, in his *The General Theory of Employment, Interest and Money* (1936), argued that there was no necessary link between savings, investment and consumption. The role of the government was to manage overall demand so that a balance was established between demand and output. If demand was too high for productive forces to meet, there would be pressure on prices. If it was deficient then resources would be idle and unemployment would result. The targets of Keynesian demand management covered inflation, employment, growth and the balance of payments.

Keynes justified active government. Government levels of spending, investment and taxation should be set to achieve the appropriate level of aggregate demand. If demand was too low (thereby encouraging additional unemployment) the Treasury should budget for a deficit and encourage state and private spending through tax cuts and/or through reduced interest rates. If demand was too high (thereby creating inflation) then it should budget for a surplus by cutting its own spending and increasing taxes and/or increasing interest rates. The post-war policy of demand management was an outstanding success – so far as employment was concerned. Between 1945 and 1970 unemployment averaged less than 3 per cent. Governments became Keynesian; a new paradigm for economic policy makers prevailed.

There is some dispute among economists as to whether Keynesian policies of demand management were responsible for the era of full employment. Research by Matthews (1968) suggests that British fiscal policy had actually been deflationary and had run a surplus on the current account. The high level of employment may have been more a product of increased investment and the long economic boom. Keynesianism may, however, have prevented deflations from being harsher than they were and it certainly was the language in which governments defined their policy.

The stop-go economy

From the early 1960s there was a growing concern in government over the performance of other economic variables. The employment question appeared to have been solved but other economic problems had not, notably industrial performance and international competitiveness. The well-known 'stop-go' cycles of economic management in the 1950s and 1960s were influenced less by the pursuit of full employment than by the protection of the balance of payments and the weakness of sterling. The system of fixed exchange rates pegged against the dollar and the status of sterling as an international currency made the government concerned to maintain the parity of the pound. But a regular by-product of policies of economic expansion was a balance of payments deficit as imports poured into the country. This in turn placed pressure on foreign currency reserves and on the exchange rate. Governments then took measures to deflate the economy as a demonstration of 'prudent' financial policies.

During the 1950s the so-called Phillips curve, named after Professor Phillips (1958), purported to demonstrate a stable relationship between the rate of inflation and unemployment. This showed that an increase in the pressure of demand was associated with a rise in prices and employment; a decrease was associated with a slowing down in price rises and an increase in unemployment. One could therefore 'trade off' price stability against economic expansion. Politicians, in other words, could manage demand by choosing between differing amounts of inflation and unemployment; it was a question of striking an acceptable balance. Gamble and Walkland (1984, p. 44) have noted that both parties accepted the overall framework and competed by offering themselves as more competent managers of the economy:

Each party claimed it could deliver higher employment, lower prices, and faster economic growth than the other. There was relatively little conflict over the objectives themselves. . . . (the trade-offs were clearly understood) . . . But in their electoral campaigns both parties preferred to claim that all the major objectives of stabilisation policy could be realized simultaneously.

Samuel Brittan stresses the continuity in economic policy when Labour returned to office in 1964 – 'whether the emphasis is on incomes policy, the regional approach to unemployment, the National Plan, the attempts to join the Common Market, the long-term regulation of Government expenditure, the idea of continuous economic relations instead of merely Budgets, or even (in embryonic form) the stress on physical "supply side" policies had already been adopted by Conservative ministers very early in the 1960s' (1971, p. 227). Further support for the consensus comes from Lord Roberthall, who served as chief economic advisor to successive Labour and Conservative Chancellors of the Exchequer between 1947 and 1961. His obituarist notes that when the Conservatives won the 1951 general election, 'it was considered automatic that Hall [as Roberthall was then known] stay on as advisor to the new government.' He claimed that he gave broadly similar advice, regardless of the chancellor, as 'he was so often in broad harmony with those whom he was advising' (Anthony Seldon, obituary of Lord Roberthall in the *Independent*, 22 September 1988).

The 1950s was the decade of full – some would now say over-full – employment. In 1955 the Conservative Government increasingly called for wage restraint if inflation was to be controlled. Its paper, *Economic Implications of Full Employment* (1956), restated the dilemma which had been recognized in the 1944 White Paper and which later governments were to use as a justification for incomes policy. It warned that the unions should not use their bargaining strengths without regard for the effects on levels of inflation and unemployment. Harold Macmillan's phrase, 'most of our people *have never had it so good*' (our emphasis), is now famous. Less well-known are the words which followed in his speech in Bedford in 1957:

What is beginning to worry some of us is 'Is it too good to be true?' or perhaps I should say 'Is it too good to last?' For amidst all this prosperity, there is one problem that has troubled us – in one way or another – ever since the war. It's the problem of rising prices. Our constant concern today is – can prices be steadied while at the same time we maintain full employment in an expanding economy? Can we control inflation? This is the problem of our time.

The decline of Keynesian optimism

In the late 1960s it was clear that the British economy was suffering from increasing amounts of both inflation and unemployment. The Phillips curve relationship had broken down. The term 'stagflation' referred to the combination of low growth with rising unemployment and inflation. Research also showed that it was taking larger injections of demand to reduce unemployment at each stage of the economic cycle and that at each stage the relationship between levels of unemployment and inflation was deteriorating. (table 3.1). Reflation by increased government spending helped to increase employment for a time but it also caused inflation to accelerate and eventually left unemployment higher at the next down-turn in

Table 3.1   The worsening economic performance

Government	Average annual increase in retail prices (%)	Average number of UK adults unemployed, seasonally adjusted
Conservative 1951–64	3.5	330,000
Labour 1964–70	4.5	500,000
Conservative 1970–4	9.0	750,000
Labour 1974–9	15.0	1,250,000

the cycle. Something of an intellectual crisis developed at the heart of Keynesian economics.

Injecting monetary demand at a rate above that of productivity growth produced higher inflation. Governments tried to control inflation by resorting to incomes policy and to relieve the balance of payments pressures by deflating the domestic economy. Between 1959 and 1979 all governments experimented with periods of incomes policy. At the same time, there was a conscious attempt to extend the role of government in the real economy to boost economic growth. This began what David Marquand (1988a) has called the 'hands-on phase' of Keynesianism, as governments tried to improve the supply side of the economy.

The last attempt by a government to pursue full employment was made by the 1970 Heath Government. In 1971 and 1972 it expanded the money supply and reflated the economy through greater public spending when unemployment threatened to break the 1 million mark. This expansion was accompanied in 1972 by a statutory prices and incomes policy to control inflation. The sharp rise in Arab oil prices in 1973 and the collapse of Mr Heath's prices and incomes policy in 1974 fuelled inflation. The worsening terms of the trade-off under the Heath Government are seen in table 3.2.

Table 3.2 The worsening economic performance

Year	Retail price index (% increase over previous year)	Wages and salaries per unit of output (% increase over previous year)	Unemployed including school leavers: UK	
			'000s	% change over previous year
1970	+6.4	+9.4	555	+7.1
1971	+9.4	+9.0	724	+30.4
1972	+7.1	+8.8	804	+11.0
1973	+9.2	+6.4	575	−28.5
1974	+16.0	+23.9	542	−5.7

Source: Pliatsky, 1984, p. 110

In 1974–5 the wage round reached an average of 26 per cent and inflation reached 25 per cent. Stopping inflation became the primary goal of stabilization policy. The new Labour Government had returned to power in 1974 as the party most identified with full employment but was faced with this major inflationary crisis and eventually negotiated an incomes policy with the TUC in June 1975.

More significant in the long term was the revolution in economic policy and the rejection of Keynesianism. In 1975 Denis Healey's budget abandoned the commitment to plan for full employment. It chose to reduce, instead of increase, the budget deficit, in spite of an unemployment total of over half a million. Keynesian orthodoxy would have dictated that the budget reduce taxes and/or increase public spending. In his first speech to the party conference as party leader in 1976 James Callaghan boldly stated the new thinking.

We used to think that you could just spend your way out of recession and increase employment only by cutting taxes and boosting government expenditure ... it only worked by injecting bigger doses of inflation into the economy followed by a higher level of unemployment at the next step ... the option [of spending yourself out of a recession] no longer exists.

The switch in policy was confirmed by the 1976 IMF rescue package for sterling. The government was now forced to reduce the public sector borrowing requirements (by £1 billion for 1977–8 and £1.5 billion in 1978–9), cash limit many of its programmes, and set targets for money supply. The policy had some success. Inflation was lowered to 8 per cent by 1978, although it was rising again when Labour left office in 1979. But unemployment doubled from 1975 to 1977, from 700,000 to 1.4 million and then fell a little by 1979.

New Right economics

Economists differed about post-Keynesian policies for achieving high employment and stable prices. Neo-Keynesians wished to pursue economic growth but curb inflation by an incomes policy. The Cambridge School, identified with the university's department of applied economics, argued that since Britain's manufacturing was uncompetitive the home market would have to be protected by import controls and, if necessary, an incomes policy. The call for import controls achieved some influence in the left wing of the Labour Party. But the most influential response came from a school of monetarists, known as the New Right. Inspired by Milton Friedman of Chicago University, and Frederick von Hayek, both Nobel prize-winners for economics, they argued that the key to reducing inflation was to control the money supply. Friedman claimed that inflation was always a monetary phenomenon and that incomes policy were thus irrelevant. Policymakers also had to take account of *expectations* of inflation. There was only one rate of unemployment consistent with a constant rate of inflation – the non-accelerating inflation rate of unemployment (what economists called NAIRU). If the government expanded demand to push unemployment below this rate, then inflation would continue to rise, as popular expectations of inflation were revised upwards. The ideas of Friedman received an airing in Britain in the late 1960s in the columns of Peter Jay, the economics editor of *The Times*, and Samuel Brittan, the economics commentator of the *Financial Times*. Friedman's and Hayek's ideas were also promoted in the seminars and pamphlets of the free market publishing house, the Institute of Economic Affairs.

At a time when decision-makers were faced with recession, when the main economic variables – inflation, employment, growth and balance of payments – were all deteriorating, and when Keynesianism was discredited, there was a clear need for new ideas and instruments of policy. Rather than 'fine-tuning' the economy and trying to influence demand and employment, government was urged to settle for a more modest task – one that was actually in its power. Controlling the money supply was a task which government could do. If wage bargainers settled for inflationary wage increases this would result in an increase in unit costs, a loss of competitiveness and the destruction of jobs. But if they believed that the government would not print more money then in time they would adapt their behaviour accordingly.

Some commentators also argued that the inflationary consequences of stimulating demand would 'overload' the economy and threaten the country's political stability. Both Samuel Brittan (1975) and Peter Jay claimed that party competition – an essential feature of democracy – raised unfulfillable expectations among voters and stopped governments taking necessary but unpopular measures. Vote-seeking politicians regarded the full employment commitment as crucial but promoting it only accelerated inflation. This 'contradiction' in the democratic political economy would undermine prosperity and liberal democracy itself. In the end, people would turn to authoritarian leaders in the hope of restoring financial stability.

Yet New Right thinkers like Sir Keith Joseph also claimed that 'monetarism is not enough.' Joseph argued that the government should also adopt a number of 'supply side' measures to restore the enterprise economy. It should cut direct taxation, encourage work incentives and promote labour mobility through lower welfare benefits and weakening the powers of trade unions. Above all, governments should disclaim responsibility for maintaining full employment. Only the two sides of industry could achieve that by accepting lower wages and salaries and making their products more competitive. Sir Keith also claimed that some unemployment was voluntary and that the official unemployment figures actually exaggerated the number of those genuinely seeking work. The official figures needed to be reduced to take account of the work-shy, the unemployable, those engaged in the black economy but registered as unemployed, and those who were shifting between jobs. Expanding demand was no answer for these types of unemployment which did not arise from deficient demand. For Sir Keith, the economic role of government was to control the money supply and reduce taxation and government borrowing. Only then would inflation be squeezed out of the system.

The new Conservative Right divided between those who attacked Keynes for misdirecting post-war economic policy and those who claimed that Keynes had been misunderstood. In fact Keynes was not indifferent to inflation, the money supply or the problems that collectivism might pose for individual liberty. Sir Keith Joseph claimed that 'what was said and done in his [Keynes's] name has been quite different . . . from what Keynes wrote. It seems likely that he would have disowned most of the allegedly Keynesian remedies made in his name and which have caused so much harm' (1975, p. 25).

The theories of the New Right were given further intellectual support by the work of Roger Bacon and Walter Eltis, *Britain's Economic Problems: Too Few Producers* (1975). This book observed that, in recent years, there had been a substantial shift of resources and workers from market to non-market goods and services. By 'market' they meant goods and services which are sold for a price and are largely in the private sector. By 'non-market' they referred to those goods and services provided by the government out of general revenue. They argued that the growth of the public sector was 'crowding out' investment and employment in the market sector and – in so far as it was financed by taxes – was a drain on the market sector. In fact the broad distinction between the productive private sector and the unproductive public sector is a crude one. Many public goods and services are productive (however indirectly, good education and health care may improve the performance of the workforce) and many are also marketed. The actual growth in public sector employment was rather modest, from 23.5 per cent to 26 per cent of the total workforce between 1964 and 1974. Some of the increase was a response to demographic pressures for public spending, such as the growing number of old age pensioners and school age children. Moreover, as an explanation of Britain's economic decline the Bacon and Eltis thesis failed to take account of such inconvenient facts as that Britain's relative economic decline long preceded the growth of the public sector, and that many other countries with impressive rates of economic growth had also experienced growth in the public sector. No matter: the thesis of *Too Few Producers* was convenient for those Conservatives who wanted to reduce public spending and employment as a means of curbing inflation and advancing political freedom. Interestingly, some Labour ministers, including the chancellor, Mr Healey, lent support to the broad thrust of the analysis.

Public spending overload

Public spending was singled out as a major cause of the problems of inflation, exessive state intervention, high taxation and the lack of economic enterprise. Between 1959 and 1964 public spending was about a third of GDP, rising to 38.5 per cent in 1972–3 (table 3.3). It then went out of control, increasing as a proportion of GDP to 45.0 per cent in 1974–5. The Public Expenditure Spending Committee (PESC) system of planning government spending over a five-year period was not designed to cope with *political* decisions to let public sector incomes rise as sharply as in 1974–5 or with the 'social wage' costs of the Social Contract (food and housing subsidies, increases in welfare benefits, etc. – see p. 64). The next year spending peaked at 45.4 per cent and then fell back to 40 per cent when Labour left office in 1979. Until 1976–7 the outturn on public spending usually exceeded that planned by governments, which had usually made spending commitments in anticipation of rates of economic growth which did not materialize. (It is worth noting, however, that other Western states experienced similar growth rates in public spending.) There was a tax backlash in these years, as voters in a number of states switched their support to parties which promised tax reductions. Indeed, this was an important part of the Conservative's appeal in 1979.

Reducing the rise in public spending became an acid test of the prudence of economic policy and of the authority of government. Sir Keith Joseph had public spending and the government's full employment commitment in mind in 1974 when he complained that Britain was over-governed, over-spent, over-taxed and over-borrowed: 'The path to Benn is paved with thirty years of interventions, thirty years of good intentions, thirty years of disappointments.' Under Mrs Thatcher the Conservatives were in favour of cutting back the public sector. But Labour ministers were also increasingly aware of the resistance of skilled workers to the higher taxes required to pay for public spending. It was a Labour minister who told local authorities in 1975 that 'the party is over' for public spending. Significantly, the minister, Mr Crosland, had

Table 3.3   Public spending as proportion of GDP in 1981-2 prices

Year	Proportion
1959	33.1
1964	33.9
1970–1	37.7
1973–4	39.9
1974–5	45.0
1975–6	45.4
1976–7	43.0
1977–8	39.3
1978–9	40.4
1979–80	43.8
1982–3	43.8
1987–8	42.7

Source: adapted from Pliatzky, 1984, p. 218

previously been the most articulate advocate of state spending. The Labour Right had favoured high public spending as a means of promoting equality; after 1975 it feared that the rise was damaging the economy. Though the Labour Left now promoted public spending both for welfare and to reflate the economy, belief in the beneficence of public spending had passed its peak by 1979. The party's leaders differed in their estimation of the value of the public sector – but they were at one in arguing that there had to be limits to its size.

The end of full employment

In its 1979 manifesto the Conservative Party made no mention of full employment. It promised to curb inflation by controlling government borrowing and the money supply, to encourage incentives by cutting direct tax and tackling the power of trade unions, and to restrict total public spending to levels compatible with its other goals of lower taxes and government borrowing. In his first Budget Sir Geoffrey Howe stated that public expenditure was at the heart of the country's economic problems. In its first public spending programme, the government planned for a 5 per cent reduction in public spending (a substantial cut-back on that planned by the last Labour Government) in the following four years. (In fact there was a growth of 8 per cent in real terms.) In a letter to the House of Commons Treasury and Civil Service Committee in June 1980, the Treasury spelt out the new orthodoxy. Reduction of inflation was its priority and 'a commitment to high employment . . . could not be met.' In addition, 'The Government has deliberately not set its targets in terms of . . . price stability and high output and employment, because these are not within its direct control.' This was the first formal announcment of the abandonement of the employment objective. Sir Leo Pliatzky, a senior civil servant at the time, has recently commented: 'there had ceased to be any trade-off in government policies between the counter-inflation objective and the employment objective. The counter-inflation objective was overwhelming.' (1984, p. 172). As the enterprise economy recovered the government claimed that unemployment would fall – if people adapted to the new conditions, particularly in negotiating lower wage settlements. No action showed the demise of Keynesianism in government circles more dramatically than Sir Geoffrey Howe's 1981 budget. In spite of the recession the Chancellor produced a deflationary package, increasing taxes by £4 billion, to protect his public sector borrowing requirement. Between 1979 and 1983 the government nearly halved the budget deficit from 5 per cent of GDP to 2.7 per cent. This was a tighter fiscal stance than that of other West European countries. A result was that the economy was driven deeper into recession and unemployment soared. The government inherited a figure of 5.4 per cent unemployment (1.2 million) but by January 1982 the figures had more than doubled to 12.7 per cent and 3 million. In the same period GDP fell by 6 per cent and manufacturing output by some 20 per cent.

One feature of government policy led directly to an increase in unemployment. North Sea oil meant that economic management was no longer plagued by balance of payments constraints. Yet, paradoxically, oil made the pound an attractive currency on the international market and the rapid appreciation of sterling made British exports less competitive. In the first Thatcher term something like a third of manufacturing plant and jobs was lost – yet the government kept interest rates high to support the exchange rate. A strong pound became a crucial plank of the anti-inflation strategy, notwithstanding its disastrous effects on employment.

Government spokesmen have produced different explanations for the loss of jobs. At first they blamed recalcitrant trade unions, particularly restrictive practices, over-staffing and excessive wage settlements. They pointed to the international recession which drove up unemployment in many countries, although they failed to explain why unemployment increased so much more rapidly in Britain than elsewhere. They have also argued that Britain has been under greater pressure for jobs because of the 'bulge' of young people coming into the labour market in the 1980s. Moreover, they have claimed that more jobs have been created in Britain than in any other state in the European Community since 1983. Indeed by July 1988 the unemployment figures had fallen for 24 months consecutively – to 2.3 million and 7.5 per cent. These, however, are still nearly twice as high as the figures the Conservatives inherited in 1979.

The Thatcher governments have several times redefined the categories of the unemployed and removed some groups which were previously counted in the figures. The most significant changes have been to exclude men over 60 and to count only those claiming benefits and looking for work instead of those registered as unemployed. This last change has excluded mainly married women seeking work but not entitled to benefit. All told, the revisions have reduced the official figures by at least 500,000. Although full employment has been abandoned as a goal of macro-economic policy the government is still keenly aware of how rising levels of unemployment affect its popularity. In the 1980s surveys have regularly shown that the public regards this as the most important issue. The government has introduced numerous schemes for adult retraining and job creation, including the Community Programme, the Enterprise Allowance Scheme, the Voluntary Projects Programme and many Youth Training Schemes.

In the 1987 election Conservatives claimed that their

policies were bringing unemployment levels down. This was achieved not by pursuing full employment as an explicit goal but by creating 'the conditions in which business can prosper and create new jobs' (Conservative manifesto). In its manifesto Labour promised to reduce unemployment by 1 million in the first two years. This would be done by the classic Keynesian methods of greater capital expenditure in the public sector and the creation of 300,000 extra jobs in the health and education services. In an echo of the old corporatism, Labour would also conduct a national economic assessment, with employers and trade unions, to decide on measures to promote national recovery. Such pump-priming promised a return to the policies of the pre-Thatcher period and differed from those practised by the last Labour Government under Mr Callaghan. It was an appeal to the values of the earlier consensus and one that, in the changed circumstances of the 1980s, failed to make much of an impact.

4 The Role of the Trade Unions

The victory of the Labour Party in 1945 was also a victory for the trade unions. The party had grown out of the trade union movement ('out of its bowels' according to Ernest Bevin); the party leadership owed its position largely to the support of the trade unions; the unions contributed massively (and would soon do even more so) to the party's financial and organizational resources. Before the war the unions had not been regarded as an estate of the realm. In 1921 and 1926 they had actually flirted with direct action. High unemployment, hostile legislation and, after 1931, an unsympathetic government had weakened their position. All this changed in 1940.

The labour connection

The symbol of trade unionism's place in wartime politics was, of course, Ernest Bevin, the former general secretary of Britain's largest union, the Transport and General Workers' Union (TGWU). Brought into government by Churchill in 1940 as minister of labour in order to make organized labour part of the war effort, Bevin became the central figure in the 1945 Attlee Government. The fact that he was foreign secretary in no way lessened his union connections and interests. Trade unionists formed a major part of the personnel of the new administration and a total of 29 out of 81 government posts went to known sponsored MPs (Allen, 1960, p. 264). Out of the 393 MP's elected, 120 were sponsored by trade unions, including five members of the new Cabinet. Bevin's successor as minister of labour was George Isaacs, the chairman of the TUC (Pelling 1971, pp. 221–2).

Not surprisingly the new government acted quickly to protect and advance the institutional resources of trade unionism. One of the very first pieces of legislation was the repeal of the 1927 Trade Disputes and Trade Unions Act which had been passed by the Conservatives in the aftermath of the General Strike. The act had severely restricted union rights. It outlawed sympathy strikes, made picketing much more difficult, prohibited civil service unions from affiliating to the Trade Union Congress (let alone the Labour Party) and forced union members wanting to pay the political levy to contract in. All the measures in the act were abolished. Another early measure was the 1946 decasualization of the Dock Labour Act, which satisfied a long term grievance of the TGWU.

But other government measures went much further than a simple guarantee of unions' civil rights. In July 1944 the TUC had set out its post-war objectives in its *Interim Report on the Post War Reconstruction*. This document established an agenda for economic management that stressed the need to extend public ownership and the unions' determination to have 'a decisive share in the actual control of the economic life of the nation' (Barnes and Reid, 1980, p. 12). The government subsequently delivered by nationalizing the iron and steel, coal, gas and electricity industries, the railways, and road haulage. During the war, the TUC had been involved in national bodies such as the National Joint Advisory Council to the Ministry of Labour, the Central Production Advisory Council and innumerable regional and local supervisory bodies for industry. The number of government committees on which trade unions were represented rose from 12 in 1939 to 60 in 1948–9 (Allen, 1960, p. 34). The unions were consulted about the content of the nationalisation package and about the new management structures it created. Emanuel Shinwell, minister of fuel, consulted the TUC General Council and the National Union of Mineworkers about appointments to the National Coal Board and selected one person nominated by each (Pelling, 1971, p. 223).

Though the trade unions did not determine the course of government economic policy between 1945 and 1951, there can be no doubt that their leadership was in general very cooperative. In February 1948 a TUC emergency conference backed by 5 million votes to 2 million the wage freeze that the Chancellor of the Exchequer, Stafford Cripps, thought necessary. In 1945 the General Council had agreed to a continuation of the wartime Order 1305 which greatly restricted the right to strike and provided for compulsory arbitration, and union leaders subsequently gave full support to the strong measures (such as bringing in troops) that the government used to defeat a rash of unofficial strikes in the docks in 1948 and 1949. The strong anti-Communism that was at the root of this support, and that led, for example, in 1949 to the TGWU ban on Communists' holding union office, spilled over into trade union backing for the foreign and defence policy that led to the creation of the Atlantic Alliance.

Thus the trade unions appeared to be part of the new post-war political order – linked by ties of loyalty, belief, personnel and interest to the Attlee Government. Between 1945 and 1947 the number of trade unionists paying the political levy rose by approximately 2 million and union contributions grew from 80 per cent (1945) to 96 per cent (1955) of Labour's election funds. Within internal Labour Party politics the major unions used the block vote system with which they dominate the party conference, to support the Parliamentary Labour Party (PLP) leadership against the Left.

Yet the very fact that the unions were so closely linked to the Labour Party suggests that they were not, to use Middlemas's phrase, one of the 'governing institutions'. After all, trade unions had been incorporated into the decision-making process in the First World War and this had not prevented a breakdown in communication as soon as party politics reasserted itself. There was some evidence that the Conservative Party was not prepared to accept the panoply of rights which the unions had achieved after 1945. The *Industrial Charter* is often, and rightly, seen as a symbol of the Conservative acceptance of a changed political economy; but it is worth pointing out that its provisions included proposals to restore contracting-in and to prohibit any linkages between civil service trade unions and political parties (Hoffman, 1964, pp. 150–1). In 1947 a Conservative party conference resolution regretted the 'subservience of the present Socialist Government to the TUC', and, in the run-up to the 1950 and 1951 elections, party rhetoric became more free market in its hostility to the public sector economy and to the planning mechanism on which trade unions were represented (Gamble, 1974, p. 147). Shortly before the 1951 election Churchill spoke out against the closed shop that allowed, for example, Durham County Council to insist that all its workers belong to the appropriate union. (Seldon, 1981, p. 570, n. 71). Another senior Tory, David Maxwell Fyfe, raised the possibility of new trade union legislation (Seldon, 1981, pp. 18–19).

What needs to be explained therefore is why the trade unions remained agents of the political consensus after the defeat of the Labour Government in 1951. It is important to remember that this is a different question from that which seeks to discover why they remained powerful political actors for a much longer period, since the case of the early 1970s (or of Communist trade unionism in Fifth Republic France) shows that trade union power can exist in a hostile political culture. The point about Britain is that both political and administrative elites accepted the desirability of working with, rather than against, the trade union leadership right up to 1979, with the single exception of the first two years of the Heath administration (1970–2). Obviously there were on occasion strong disagreements over particular aspects of economic management but few politicians challenged the belief that if there could not be a consensus on policy there must be one on process. A number of reasons for this can be advanced, some of which relate to the whole post-war period, while others apply only to its first 20 years.

The first reason is the 'climate of opinion' and relates to the leftward shift in public opinion that occurred during the war. In a culture that came to accept W. H. Auden's view of the 1930s as the low, dishonest decade, trade unions acquired legitimacy as defenders of the underprivileged and partners in the fight against Fascism. The Home Front ethos that existed in both wars did not disappear in 1945 as it had done in 1918, for the simple reason that 1945 was to presage not a return to 'normalcy' but a 'New Society'. In this climate the record of the inter-war Conservative party in its dealings with trade unions was distinctly unfavourable and Churchill in particular was vulnerable to the charge of union-bashing, because of his allegedly aggressive anti-union behaviour in Tonypandy (1912) and the General Strike of 1926. (As late as 1978 Mr Callaghan could taunt Churchill's grandson in the House of Commons with 'his family's historic vendetta against the miners'.)

One aspect of the post-war reorganization of the Conservative Party was an attempt to build up a trade union section and the creation, in 1947, of a Central Trade Union Advisory Committee. More importantly, the leadership went out of its way to stress its acceptance of, and commitment to, free trade unionism. The party reasserted its nineteenth-century role (identified with Disraeli) in protecting unions from the harshness of judicial *laissez-faire* and assured them that there would be no road back to 1927 (Gamble, 1974, p. 46). Nationalization was attacked in the party's 1951 *Campaign Guide* precisely because it created a conflict between the unions' duty to defend their members' interests and their allegiance to a democratically elected government. The political levy was not even mentioned in the *Guide* and the mild reference of Maxwell-Fyfe, the party's chief spokesman on labour affairs, to the possibility of union legislation was enough to deprive him of the post of minister of labour which he had expected. In his place Churchill appointed Walter Monckton, a non-political lawyer whose temperament was always for conciliation and who was described at the time by a fellow Conservative as 'that old oil can' (Birkenhead, 1969, p. 275). Churchill envisaged Monckton's role as one of keeping the unions sweet, and both men went out of their way to demonstrate their good intentions. Trade union leaders were invited to receptions at 10 Downing Street, their views were canvassed on a wide range of issues and ideas of further legislation dropped.

Most importantly, Churchill and Monckton were very accommodating towards wage demands in the public sector. In

1952, after the government initially referred back various Wage Council pay awards, the TUC intervened with Churchill and obtained a promise that such awards would not be interfered with in the future. The following year, a threatened railway strike was avoided by late night union–government negotiations in which the National Union of Railwaymen's demands were largely met. (Birkenhead, 1969, p. 292). Although such deals did not go uncriticized within the party, the overriding political goal of the leadership was not to destabilize the structure that had been created during and after the war (Beer, 1969, pp. 319–51). After the 1953 railway strike was averted George Isaacs, Monckton's Labour predecessor as Minister of Labour, paid him a glowing tribute.

This cooperation can also be shown in areas other than that of pay settlements. A major characteristic of post-war European political settlements was an extended role for government in economic management. This involved not simply the extension of public ownership but also the attempt to shape – indeed to plan – the overall development of the economy. One part of this process (and an important one that differentiated Western democracy from the command economies being established in Eastern Europe) was to involve economic actors, and that meant unions, in a democratic process. This could work at company level, as in the German co-partnership known as *mitbestimmung*, or at national level, as in the sectoral commissions that formed the core of the French Planning Commissariat. National planning did not survive for long in post-war Britain and the replacement of physical controls by Keynesian methods reduced both government's ability to intervene and the role of collective planning boards. Nevertheless, the return of the Conservatives in 1951 in no way presaged a decline in the role of trade unions in the existing consultative and executive structures at both national and local level. The Conservatives were even more willing to appoint trade unionists to consultative committees than Labour had been (Allen, 1960, p. 34) – unionists sat on 81 government committees in the years 1953–4 and 65 in 1957–8. Beer (1969) claims that by 1958 the trade unions had achieved parity of representation with employers on some 850 committees, including the

National Production Advisory Council and all the economic planning boards. Writing in 1956 Anthony Crosland observed, 'One cannot imagine today a deliberate offensive alliance between Government and employers against the unions. . . . Instead the atmosphere in Whitehall is almost deferential, the desire not to give offence positively ostentatious.'

It can be argued that after 1955 the idea of the 'positive consensus' as a deliberate sharing of assumptions became weaker. To that extent the 'Indian Summer', which forms the title of Seldon's study of the 1951–55 administration, applies not just to Churchill but to the whole coalition spirit. Certainly tensions began to appear in the hitherto harmonious pattern of relations between unions and government. Various factors are relevant. In 1955 a prolonged railway strike organized by the train drivers' union (ASLEF) was the first national strike for twenty years seriously to inconvenience the public. In 1957 the number of days lost through strikes – 8.5 million – was the highest since 1926. From this period trade unions began to suffer that broad public disapproval which they have never since lost. At the same time there occurred a shift, though not a revolution, in what might be called the 'system attitudes' of important trade union leaders. The TGWU, for example, whose two leaders Bevin and then Deakin had epitomized and indeed created the 'top-down, responsible' model of trade unionism of the post-war years, was now led by Frank Cousins. His speech to the TUC Conference in 1956, in the words of one observer, sounded like the death knell of the 'certainties of the old guard of TUC leadership' (Goodman, 1979, p. 135).

Cousins stood for a more left-wing political posture than that of his predecessors as well as for a more 'democratic' (that is, decentralized) approach to union business, and in particular to wage-bargaining. Pay deals were to be imposed not by national union officials but by negotiation on the shop floor. This was correctly seen as giving power to militant shop stewards, particularly once Cousins removed the ban on Communists holding union offices. In no circumstances would the union cooperate in policies of wage restraint advocated by government. The growing radicalism of some union leaders obviously made for a more adversarial relationship with the

Conservatives – but it also posed problems for the Labour Party, both out of and in power, as Gaitskell and then Wilson would discover.

Thus from the mid-1950s onwards the trade unions came to be seen as a problem for government. Their status as national, if not actually governing, institutions remained secure; but their popularity amongst the population was in decline and they were increasingly viewed by policy makers as a hindrance to the efficient running of the economy (Taylor, 1987). What made this last point particularly serious was the increasing, almost obsessive, interest in the relatively poor performance of the British economy compared with its European rivals – inflation rates were consistently higher and levels of economic growth and investment lower. The governments' responses to this would shape the pattern of union–government relations over the next 20 years in such a way that it is possible to talk about a 'policy consensus' between the two parties. This was so even though each party when in opposition criticized the other's strategy and trade unionism became one of the chief themes in adversarial politics. The ideological assumptions and electoral interests of both Labour and Conservatives made trade union power an inevitable cause of party conflict. Yet what gave the approach its overall consistency was the shared belief amongst the parties that the conventions of the mixed economy model alone were no longer adequate, and that greater governmental involvement on the supply side was needed – the real economy must be managed and not simply massaged. The levers and techniques were available: it was a matter of getting them right.

The hidden consensus

The *de facto* consensus had three main features. The first was the need for a *national wages policy*. Although the trade union leadership had, as we have seen, acquiesced in a period of wage restraint in the late 1940s, free collective bargaining was seen as an indispensable part of free trade unionism. Yet it was always realized that free collective bargaining in circumstances of full employment had potentially inflationary consequences.

The 1944 White Paper on Employment stated: 'If . . . we are to operate with success a policy for maintaining a high and stable level of employment it will be essential that employers and workers should exercise moderation in wage matters.' Keynes claimed that tackling the enhanced power of the unions was an 'essentially political problem'. From 1961 that aspect of the union problem came to the forefront of British politics. Already in 1957 there had been government attempts at encouraging wage restraint, with the 1957 Council on Productivity, Prices and Incomes and the Guillebaud Commission on comparability. Much attention was paid by some economists and commentators to the success of wage policies in countries like Sweden and Holland (Barnes and Reid, 1980, p. 30). Yet in the economic crisis of 1961 the government, without consulting the unions, imposed a pay freeze in the public sector and announced that this would be followed by a permanent incomes policy, based on a 'guiding light' set by the government and aimed at encouraging wage restraint. The pause lasted nine months; the policy was dead within three. It collapsed because of government unwillingness to face the industrial and political consequences of widespread labour unrest. The trade unions refused to cooperate in the running of the National Incomes Commission, a toothless body established in July 1962 to assess the impact of pay settlements on the economy but with no power to interfere with collective bargaining (Barnes and Reid, 1980, p. 38).

The wages policy approach is a good example of the implicit rather than overt consensus between parties on one major feature of trade union power – its ability to stoke up inflation via pay settlements. The experience of the Macmillan Government would be repeated under Wilson (1966–9), Heath (1972–4) and Wilson/Callaghan (1975–9). On all four occasions, the immediate policy was made necessary by suddenly worsening economic conditions (in inflation and balance of payments) but was intended to be followed by an indefinite period of wage planning, which, however, soon broke down. By 1968 there had been seven White Papers on incomes policy in three years. Labour's links with the trade unions meant that its wages policies (statutory in 1966, non-statutory in 1976) aroused less initial protest from the unions than those of Macmillan and (particularly) Heath. Yet it remains the case that the unions did not initially seek to destroy Heath's statutory policy but that they did ultimately destroy the policies of both Wilson (1969) and Callaghan (1978). The Trades Union Congress in September 1968 passed a resolution calling for the repeal of the prices and incomes legislation by over 7 million votes to 1 million.

The second feature of the 'implicit consensus' was the *involvement of trade unions* in the formulation of macro-economic policy. The fascination with indicative planning and the more interventionist role for government that was an aspect of Conservative as well as Labour thinking in the early 1960s contributed to a desire to involve the major producer groups in economic management (One feature of the widely admired French planning mechanism was the involvement of the trade unions there in the *commissions de modernisation*. In fact, the CGT, the largest trade union in France, withdrew from the plan in the early 1960s and it certainly could not be said that planning made French unions, which had fewer resources than their British equivalents and different traditions, more 'responsible'.)

The institutional consequence of this desire for cooperation in economic management was the creation in 1962 of the National Economic Development Council. The trade unions were vital legitimizing actors in the NEDC; as a price of their cooperation they were able to obtain the assurance that the new Council would not be able to involve itself in wage discussions, or any other matters that were within the remit of collective bargaining. Its role was rather, as the 1964 Conservative manifesto said, to give 'reality to the democratic concept of planning by partnership' (Gamble and Walkland, 1984, p. 116).

Labour, of course, saw itself as the party with a genuine commitment to planning and the involvement of trade unions in economic management. Its *National Plan* of 1965 was the clearest evidence of this. But so too was the *Joint Statement of Intent on Productivity, Prices and Incomes*, signed by the Labour Government, employers and trade unions in December 1964. Mr Wilson also brought into the Cabinet the most powerful trade union leader, Frank Cousins, in an attempt to recreate the party–union axis of 1945. When Labour returned to government in 1974, it did so on the basis of a wide–ranging package of social and economic measures which had been agreed with the trade unions in a newly created TUC–Labour Party Liaison Committee and which became known as the Social Contract (see p. 64).

The 1974 agreement was obviously far removed from the 'depoliticized' planning that had been the ideal behind attempts to involve the trade unions in the NEDC. Yet government–union cooperation became a feature of the Conservative Party strategy too and gave rise to the belief that decision-making in Britain was becoming corporatist in style. In 1972, after its defeat by the miners over a pay claim, Mr Heath's Government invited the trade unions, along with employers' leaders, to a lengthy series of negotiations over the future management of the economy. Mr Heath told the 1972 Conservative Party Conference, 'the trade unions and the employers [must] share fully with the government the benefits and obligations of running the economy.' The later talks took place in the Cabinet Room at 10 Downing Street. Heath's goal was to obtain TUC consent to wage restraint in return for a commitment to faster growth and measures against inflation. In the event the talks failed. The political cost of acceding to the TUC demand for a repeal of the 1971 Industrial Relations Act and the Housing Finance Act was too high – it would not simply involve the rejection of two major pieces of the Tory programme, but dangerously underline the extent to which parliamentary government was being replaced by corporatist accommodation. The talks revealed, nevertheless, just how far the Conservative leadership was prepared to go in acknowledging the legitimacy of trade unions within the political process. (It is worth remembering that many trade unions leaders came to have a high regard for Mr Heath.)

The use of law

The third element in the *de facto* governing consensus reflected the same recognition of the power of trade unions and their perceived ability to affect the overall performance of the national economy. But it drew the more radical conclusion that their capacity for damage was so great that there was a need for *measures of legal restraint*. Trade unions were blamed not just for price uncompetitiveness but also for delays in production, brought about by strike-happy shop stewards. It is important to note that initially the complaint was not only, and perhaps not even primarily, about the threats that unions posed to the liberties of their individual members. What mattered more was the damage they inflicted on national economic performance. When the Labour Government came to power in 1964 it enacted legislation that protected unions' closed shop rights against an unfavourable legal judgement given in *Rookes v. Barnard*. At the same time it appointed a Royal Commission (the first such commission for 60 years) under Lord Donovan to carry out a 'high level and searching inquiry into the role of both the trade unions' and the employers' organizations in a modern society'.

The TUC General Council was allowed to nominate its own representatives, including the then general secretary, George Woodcock. The concern about industrial relations that led to the Commission continued whilst it was preparing its report; the period of its deliberations was punctuated not simply by macro-economic problems that culminated in the November 1967 devaluation but also by strikes, both official (railways, docks) and unofficial. When the Report finally appeared in June 1968 it acknowledged that the reality of trade union power lay in the localized, or informal, system of industrial relations, and that national union organizations had little influence over events. The internal politics of the Commission, however (and in particular Donovan's determination not to let the trade union representatives dissent from its conclusions) meant that it shied away from any proposal to strengthen the law against any trade unionist activities. The Report was widely seen as a failure – and attention focused on the note of dissent from the economist Andrew Shonfield, who argued that the state could not absent itself from industrial relations in the workplace. He recommended legal measures to protect people against damage caused by strike and powers of intervention for the Commission on Industrial Relations, backed by fines, to deal with inter-union disputes. Shonfield's ideas were clearly much too dangerous for a Labour government. Yet the unions' – and the government's – unpopularity made it essential for the latter to go beyond the apparently helpless passivity of the main report, particularly in an epoch when government was supposed to be dynamically interventionist.

The result was the 1969 White Paper *In Place of Strife* which envisaged a new regulatory body, the Commission on Industrial Relations (CIR), with powers to make recommendations in cases of inter-union disputes, which could then be enforced by fines. The secretary of state for employment could also impose a cooling off period in the case of unconstitutional strikes, and order a ballot of workers in those disputes which would involve a serious threat to the economy or public interest.

In Place of Strife fell victim to the weight of historical and cultural tradition in the Labour Party. It seemed to many back-benchers that turning the law on the very organizations that had created the party was an act of parricide. By the same token, the defeat of the proposals gave considerable political dividends to the Conservatives, since it not only demonstrated the utter dependence of Labour on its paymasters but vindicated the Conservatives' own belief in, and commitment to, a reform of the legislative framework within which trade unions operated. As soon as Mr Heath became leader of the Conservative Party in 1965, he set up a series of policy groups, including one on Trade Union Law and Practice (Moran, 1977, p. 59). From this would emerge the proposals of *Fair Deal at Work* (1968), which suggested that trade unions should operate in a legal framework and be held legally responsible for the actions of members, and the 1971 Industrial Relations Act. The basic idea of the legislation was to extend the traditional remedies and procedures of the civil law to the problems of industrial relations: aggrieved parties would have the right to apply to the courts for remedies – the institutional heart of the proposals lay in the National Industrial Relations Court (NIRC). All parties were to have clearly defined rights and duties. Workers were to have the right to join or refuse to join a union and the right to withdraw their labour subject only to their individual contract of employment. Among other provisions unions were to be registered, there were to be legally binding agreements and pre-strike ballots, and existing legal immunities were restricted.

The Industrial Relations Act became law in August 1971. Exactly a year later it was, in the words of Moran (p. 144), dead as a positive force in industrial relations and its repeal became a decisive stumbling block for the 1972 negotiations between government and unions described above. The TUC had been determined to destroy the act and by 1974 even the director general of the Confederation of British Industry was advocating its amendment. Attempts to use the legal penalties prescribed in the law, via the NIRC, had not only produced a heightened militancy in industrial relations, with no shortage of candidates for martyrdom; they had also led to the ludicrous situation of the Court trying to avoid the imprisonment of trade unionists guilty of offences under the laws it was its duty to enforce. The Conservative manifesto of October 1974 made only a passing reference to the Industrial Relations Act. The new Labour Government repealed all the sections of the act except those which the unions found to their benefit. The Conservatives had already indicated that they would not oppose its repeal (Stewart, 1978, p. 129).

The consequences of the failure of legislative attempts to regulate trade union activity were very different for the two parties. This explains why the policy consensus between them, which had always been more tenuous on this issue than on others, disappeared. For Labour, the failure of the Heath legislation came as a godsend. It enabled the memories of its own anti-union proposals to fade, and the highly confrontational atmosphere of the 1974 election allowed it to pose as the party that could bring industrial peace in its time.

The Wilson/Callaghan governents went out of their way to consult with trade union leaders. Under the Social Contract, negotiated by the government and the TUC, the unions obtained legislation extending job security and the closed shop. The Industrial Relations Act was repealed, welfare spending was increased, and price and dividend controls were imposed.

All this was done in return for wage restraint. Yet in its first year the policy was a flop – with wage increases reaching an annualized rate of 30 per cent . One government minister commented: 'To my mind, the only give and take in the contract was that the government gave and the unions took' (J. Barnett, 1982, p. 49). The government was more successful in 1976 and 1977 when average living standards actually fell. Jack Jones, the leader of Britain's largest union, the TGWU, was particularly supportive. He was a dominant figure like his predecessors Bevin and Deakin and was widely seen as the most powerful man in the country. (A political sketch of the time had the prime minister, Mr Callaghan, declaring at the beginning of a speech, 'When Mr Jones asked me to form a government . . .')

Both Wilson and Callaghan argued that Labour's ability to work with the unions made it the 'natural party of government', the preserver of political stability. In so doing, they were dangerously overloading what an already weakened consensus could bear. For most of the post-war period the union leaders in their relations with the Labour Party drew a distinction between political and industrial matters. They left the former to the political leaders and expected to be left alone on the latter. Preserving free collective bargaining and keeping the law out of industrial relations were major concerns for the union leaders. By the late 1960s the two biggest unions had more assertive and left-wing leaderships. Yet the 1964 and 1970 governments interfered in both policy areas. Incomes policies therefore disrupted the traditional, mutually supportive relations between Labour Party and trade union leaders.

It was also clear that the unions' response to the 1971 Act and the circumstances of the 1974 defeat of the Heath Government had greatly increased Tory hostility towards trade unionism. With Mrs Thatcher as leader and Sir Keith Joseph as chief intellectual influence, the prospects for union–Conservative collusion were probably worse than at any time since the war. 'Moncktonism' was long since dead and Heathite corporatism was fast becoming moribund.

The end of an era

The collapse of the Social Contract and the voluntary incomes policy ended a stage in post-war British history. Both incomes policy and cooperation with the unions seemed discredited. Since 1961 incomes policies had been variously statutory or non-statutory, compulsory or voluntary, and were often linked with negotiations about the broader social and economic policies of the government of the day. They were also accompanied by an array of commissions and boards to provide guidance on the implementation of policy. In many respects incomes policy is a history of the attempt to depoliticize one aspect of the union question and to curb market forces in wage bargaining. Expert or impartial commissions and norms were designed to give a voice to the consumer or the national interest, as determined by the government. Although the policies produced temporary slow-downs in inflation, the outturn of hourly wages invariably exceeded the target set, and by the second or third year the policy collapsed. The lack of central authority within the TUC, or within many unions, made it difficult to operate a long-term policy. Unions were just too unsuited to being responsible and authoritative partners for government. The postive features of corporatism found in some other countries, notably Sweden, were absent in Britain.

Yet the history of the period also raised the question of ungovernability or the lack of government authority. Industrial relations legislation had been vetoed (under Mr Wilson) or rendered ineffective (under Mr Heath) because of union opposition. The unions had flouted the courts and broken the incomes policies of Mr Heath and Mr Callaghan. In the latter case the defiance was sometimes accompanied by violent picketing. Mr Heath had lost an election in February 1974 that was, inevitably, to some degree concerned with the question, 'Who governs Britain?'. And in the 1978–9 'Winter of Discontent' the paralysis of government was obvious.

Thus the 'trade union' question became perhaps the deepest area of conflict between the two parties. The Labour Government continued to regard some form of incomes policy as an essential tool of anti-inflation policy; Conservatives had now turned for an answer to monetarism and, implicitly, unemployment. Conservatives also wanted the trade unions to operate within a legal framework whch would limit the opportunities for secondary picketing. Labour, in defence of union sensibilities, rejected such intervention, particularly on the emotive issue of picketing. Whilst Labour retained an instinctive belief in union cooperation with government, the Conservatives had by now rejected such a role.

The lack of elite agreement might not have mattered so much for the unions – or indeed for Labour – if they had been able to take the union question off the political front burner or at least to demonstrate that their own internal consensus, symbolized by the Labour Party–TUC Liaison Committee, could stil work. But they could not. All opinion polls showed that, despite an ever-growing overall union membership, the unions remained widely unpopular. More seriously, the elite accord between government and union leadership broke down in 1978, over the former's determination to maintain policies of wage restraint. In the past such breakdowns had not necessarily been politically damaging. But the circumstances of the 'Winter of Discontent' – a spate of stoppages and slow-downs, usually led from below – suggested that the government (and even the union leadership) had totally lost control. Thus the argument about governability, which had been at the origins of the unions' legitimization during and after the war, gained credibility. In 1974 the collapse of the Heath Government's political authority had worked to the immediate advantage of both Labour and the unions. But the identification of Labour with trade unionism subsequently damaged both. The immediate victim was the Labour Government, which was heavily defeated in the 1979 general election. The more long-term price was, however, paid by the trade unions themselves. They had to face a new Conservative Government determined to roll back the frontiers of union power and hostile to the assumptions on which the earlier consensus had been built.

1979: a new departure

In this light the 'Winter of Discontent' provided a heaven-sent opportunity for the Conservative Party. Having destroyed Labour's claim to have a special relationship with trade unionism and the union leaders' ability to deliver, it left the way clear for a new start. Conservatives became more outspoken in blaming the trade unions for low productivity, overstaffing, restrictive practices and strikes, particularly in the public sector. They could also point out that, despite the overwhelming pro-Labour stance of union leaders, only half their members had voted Labour in 1979. Moreover, surveys suggested that many union members supported a number of Conservative policies, particularly those for tougher legal controls on the unions. The government hoped that strict control of the money supply and its proclaimed unwillingness to bail out financially troubled firms would help to implant a more responsible outlook among wage-bargainers. In the public sector the government would give each department a cash-limited budget, including a factor for pay. If this was exceeded then either services would decline or workers would price themselves out of jobs.

For the first two years, this strategy lay in ruins because of the 'catching-up' comparability awards of the Clegg Commission for public sector pay. Over time, however, rising unemployment and fear of job losses undermined the appeal of militants and the unions. The unions also lost 3 million members between 1979 and 1983, with the large general unions involved in manufacturing industry (like the TGWU and the Amalgamated Union of Engineering workers) being particularly hard hit. In addition, the Conservatives used the law in a incremental way to redress the balance of bargaining between employers and unions. Three acts were particularly important: the Employment Acts of 1980 and 1982, and the Trade Union Act of 1984. The main effects of these acts has been to:

   make trade unions legally responsible for actions by their members and officers who breach the law;

require unions to obtain the votes of a majority of their members by secret ballot before industrial action can proceed;

make secondary picketing and sympathy strikes illegal;

require an 80 per cent favourable vote by employees before a closed shop can be established by agreement with an employer;

require union executives and officers who have a vote on the National Executive to be elected by secret ballot at least once every five years;

require unions to ballot their members every ten years over the maintenance of a political fund.

This legislation has been used by employers to weaken the power of the unions. It was used by the Messenger newspaper group in a dispute with printers in 1983 and by Rupert Murdoch's News International in its dispute in 1986 with SOGAT 82. In contrast to earlier experience, which suggested that the courts should not have a role to play in industrial relations, the government has managed to make its legislation operate. Arthur Scargill's failure to ballot National Union of Mineworkers (NUM) members before taking industrial action in the coal industry in 1984 seriously weakened the strike and helped to precipitate the breakaway of the Democratic Miners' Union in Nottinghamshire. Not only did Mr Scargill fail to gain support from other unions but nearly a third of the miners refused to support the strike. Strikes at British Leyland, British Steel and British Rail and lengthy disruptions by civil servants failed to move the government during its first term in office; and in its second term, it did not capitulate to lengthy strikes by the teaching unions, and the twelve-month strike by the NUM against pit closures ended in failure in April 1985.

There are many signs of union decline. The number of workers covered by the closed shop has fallen, as has the number of stoppages at work. The TUC has been divided over such issues as single union and no-strike deals, support for the miners' strike in 1984, union membership of the Manpower Services Commission (now Training Commission), and whether or not to boycott the government's union legislation.

More recently it has been divided over whether to participate in the government's Employment Training scheme. The government has downgraded the importance of the NEDC and has prohibited union membership for workers at the intelligence operation centre, GCHQ. It has overturned traditional methods of pay bargaining for teachers and civil servants and, directly or indirectly, carried out major job reductions in such areas of traditional union strength as the civil service and the coal, steel and shipbuilding industries. The 1988 TUC decision to boycott the Employment Training scheme is being used by some ministers as a pretext for virtually terminating all TUC membership of government committees. The decline in heavily unionized manufacturing industry and the rise in the less organised sectors of service and traditionally female employment suggests that long-term membership prospects for the unions are poor.

Here is one area in which the old consensus has clearly broken down. Unions are no longer consulted, unemployment has been used as a weapon to weaken their bargaining power, and the authority of government, not least in upholding its trade union legislation, has been amply demonstrated. The 1980s represent a very different scene from the 1970s, when much commentary dealt with the excessive power of the trade unions. The Conservatives envisage an ever-declining role in economic management for trade unions, at both macro and micro level; some right-wing commentators and politicians see them as becoming no more than what they were at their nineteenth-century beginnings, namely a form of friendly society. Labour, by contrast, is still wedded to the post-war view of trade unionism and is pledged to repeal some of the post-1979 legislation, notably on picketing. At the end of the 1980s, it is difficult to see how a new consensus may be forged on the role of trade unions although it is abundantly clear that the old one is dead.

5 The Welfare State

By 1914 the welfare state was already on the British political agenda. The state provided benefits for some citizens in old age, ill health and unemployment. Whereas pensions were non-contributory and means tested, the national insurance benefits were contributory but not means tested. Provision in Britain, however, ran behind that in the authoritarian German state, a reminder that social welfare and political democracy do not necessarily go hand in hand. In Germany welfare provision was introduced in the late nineteenth century as a trade-off against social democracy. The government hoped that by introducing measures to alleviate social and economic distress it would dampen working-class demands for political control. The example of the United States, where levels of provision have lagged behind those of Europe, is further evidence of the non-convergence of universal suffrage and collective social welfare provision.

Origins

As with public ownership the notion of a welfare state and a national health service had existed for many years. Soon after the end of the 1914–18 war the government introduced housing and unemployment insurance with little opposition. As C. L. Mowat explains: 'The reasons are clear enough. There were ancient and modest precedents for both bills. The experience of the war had prepared the country for them. And the immediate need for action which only the state seemed capable of swept aside all discussion of principle' (Mowat, 1955, p. 43). Thereafter there was a modest expansion, such as the introduction of widows' and orphans' pensions and extensions of entitlement to unemployment benefit. In 1913 total central and local government spending on social services was a quarter of all public expenditure (covering unemployment benefits and relief, old age pensions, widows' and orphans' pensions, public assistance, national health insurance, education, housing, hospitals and child welfare); by 1935 it was a third (Mowat, p. 497). But by 1939 only half the population (largely wage-earners) were covered by national health insurance. Numerous surveys before 1939 had already shown that the interruptions of earnings, usually through unemployment, or having a large number of children, were major causes of poverty. Bentley Gilbert's masterly history of social policy argues that in the inter-war years Britain's political leaders agreed 'almost unconsciously' that the state would have to guarantee a national minimum to its citizens. This was 'a private political consensus by the end of the 1930s' (Gilbert, 1970, p. vii). The necessary action to consolidate the various schemes was to be Beveridge's accomplishment.

The 1939–45 war, like that of 1914–18, was important in advancing the case for welfare in Britain. The experience enhanced the sense of social solidarity, alerted many of the better off to the extent of poverty and hardship and, so some historians claim, encouraged the notion of a contract between people and government. The people had sacrificed much in the struggle against Hitler and, in return, expected the government to produce a better post-war society. During the war the government was already helping with supplementary pensions, supply of milk to mothers and babies, and school milk and meals for all schoolchildren. It also passed the Butler Education Act (1944) which provided free schooling for all up to the age of 15.

Beveridge

The Beveridge Report was something of a historical accident. The wartime government had not anticipated the extent of Beveridge's proposals. It was concerned to meet trade union demands for compensation against industrial disease and accidents, not least because it sought wage restraint from labour. It was also under pressure to iron out anomalies in welfare and to integrate the various schemes. A committee was therefore appointed under Sir William Beveridge with a remit to examine existing schemes of social insurance and allied services and make recommendations. His review of social security, *Report on Social Insurance and Allied Services*, was produced in 1942. Beveridge wanted to introduce a minimum level of income for all and a scheme which would combat the 'giants' of 'Want, Disease, Ignorance, Squalor, and Idleness'. He proposed that existing schemes for pensions, unemployment and sickness benefits be consolidated into a universal national insurance scheme, covering people 'from cradle to grave', as Churchill said. Instead of making benefits subject to a means test, flat-rate benefits would be paid as of right in return for flat-rate contributions. There would also be a safety net of means-tested national assistance benefits for those not covered by insurance. Essentially, the government was being asked to guarantee each adult a minimum income, regardless of individual circumstances.

Support for the Beveridge plan in the House of Commons was widespread and there was also a favourable public reaction. At the time the support from Labour and Conservative back-benchers annoyed Churchill. He was concentrating all his energies on the defeat of Hitler and he did not want public attention to be distracted from that primary objective. He also thought that the plan was far too ambitious and financially imprudent. In the end, however, political considerations forced him to give way. It also seemed clear that the public would not be appeased by anything less. This was the moment when the idea of a contract between government and people was being forged: there was to be no repeat of the betrayal of post-1919, when the promised 'homes fit for heroes' remained unbuilt.

It is important to realize that Beveridge's ideas were part of a comprehensive plan for welfare. He assumed that there would be a national health service, full employment (though in formulating his plan unemployment was assumed to be 8.5 per cent) and family or child allowances. He also insisted that his scheme be based on insurance, so that people would retain the incentive to do more for themselves and their families. People should not get something for nothing; a benefit was an earned entitlement, which did not therefore undermine self-respect. The provision of uniform benefits was also crucial for the development of equality and social citizenship (rights to a job, decent housing and schooling, and protection against the economic costs of ill health, old age and unemployment), aspirations that the Second World War had done much to develop.

The new welfare state rested on two planks. One was a comprehensive health service, the other the provision of services to combat primary want. The next section of this chapter examines the creation of the NHS.

The National Health Service

A major part of the state's provision of welfare was the National Health Service. This was established by legislation in 1946 and came into operation in June 1948. Rudolf Klein (1983) argues that the service had several notable features. It was the first health system in any Western country to provide free medical care for the population; it was the only social service in Britain which catered for the entire population; and it made equality into an ethical imperative, for its declared objective was to achieve equity in the delivery of health care.

The idea of a comprehensive national health service was not new. A number of reports in the inter-war years, notably the Dawson Report (1920) and a Royal Commission on National Health Insurance (1926), pointed in this direction. By 1939, Klein argues, there already existed a consensus for a national scheme, 'dictated, as it were, by the logic of circumstances, rather than by the ideology of politicians or the demands of pressure groups' (p. 3). In the inter-war years local authorities had gained increased powers to provide hospital services for growing numbers of patients. But policy-makers felt that there was too much variation in the quality of treatment and many voluntary hospitals were facing economic difficulties. The stimulus of war, the problems of the 1500 or so hospitals run by local authorities and voluntary organizations, and the fact that about half of the population was not covered by national insurance, all encouraged reformers to consolidate the service into a national and universal one. The wartime government accepted the need for action and in its White Paper of 1944 proposed a national health service, with a substantial role reserved for the local authorities.

It fell to Aneurin Bevan, as minister of health in the 1945 Labour Government, to produce a new system. Two features of this scheme are worthy of note. First, the government decided to nationalize the hospitals rather than allow local authorities to run them. Bevan defended a national system on the grounds that this would best provide equal treatment across the country. This was carried despite the objection of a number of ministers, notably Herbert Morrison, who wanted a continuing role for local authorities on the grounds that this would facilitate local participation and democratic accountability. The removal of hospitals, along with responsibility for gas, electricity and income maintenance programmes, spelt a substantial reduction in the role of local authorities. Secondly, in contrast to the system subsequently adopted in many other Western states, Bevan rejected the insurance principle of funding the service. Under such a scheme entitlement to health care would follow the payment of contributions. Instead, the service was to be provided by the state free to the consumer; health was seen as a public good and one which the state should assume responsibility for delivering. Leaving aside the debate about whether the National Health Service was founded primarily as a measure of administrative convenience or of socialism, it is worth noting that such values as equality of treatment, the assumption of costs by the community or Exchequer and the avoidance of direct payments by patients all furthered collectivist and egalitarian ideals.

Welfare statutes

1945   Family Allowances Act, made available out of general
       taxation
1946   National Insurance Act – benefits for the unemployed,
       sick, retired and widows
1948   National Assistance Act, to provide benefits for those
       who did not have a complete record of contributions
1948   National Health Service established to provide free
       medical services.

Insurance would have involved an earmarked and assured
sum for health. As the service was financed out of general taxation, the minister of health had to bargain with the Treasury
and compete for finance with other services like education and
defence. According to the official historian of the National
Health Service, it was not realized that this step would elevate
the Health Service into a 'sensitive political issue' (Webster,
1988, p. 34). The Conservative attitude towards the National
Health Service showed greater continuities with the past than
did their stance in other areas of welfare provision.

The creation and consolidation of the welfare state was not
the work of any one political party. Most historians have
regarded two groups of actors as significant in its rise. One is
the group of *administrative rationalists* (such as Beveridge, the
Fabians and civil servants) who were interested in efficient,
cost-effective schemes *within* the existing political and economic system. The other is the *social democratic intellectuals* (such
as Tawney, Titmuss and Townsend) whose research and
writings made the case for a more equal society. The latter,
through membership of either Labour Party policy groups or
advisory bodies, were important participants in the policy
community. Many Conservatives – particularly the Tory
Reform group – supported the Beveridge proposals, though
some were critical of the costs. Although the Conservative
manifesto of 1945 promised a 'comprehensive health service'
and a social security system based on Beveridge in the eyes of
the public Labour was seen as the party more committed to
erecting a welfare state. It was Labour which managed to hijack
Beveridge (himself a Liberal).

For some 20 years there existed a consensus among policy-makers on the desirability of welfare and a general satisfaction about its performance across the front benches of the two main parties. Support for welfare was good politics. Conservatives could point to the strand of Tory paternalism and their concern for the condition of the people, going back to Disraeli and even earlier. Labour could see the welfare state as an expression of its ideals of social justice and fellowship. Yet there were still sharp differences of rhetoric between the two parties. Conservative discussion of welfare was couched in terms of equality of opportunity, protecting the interests of the taxpayer, and advancing values of thrift, self-reliance and enterprise. Labour, on the other hand, talked about fairness, compassion and social justice (MacGregor, 1981, p. 124). At general elections in the 1950s Labour regularly boasted of its post-1945 welfare reforms and warned that the Conservatives would, if given the opportunity, bring a return to the inter-war conditions of poverty and insecurity. Labour's 1955 election manifesto stated: 'Through the National Health Service and National Insurance the Labour Government began to abolish the fear of old age, sickness and disablement which haunted working class life before the war.' As we have seen, charges that the Conservatives would run down the welfare state were not borne out, and the period 1951 to 1964 saw a substantial increase in spending on the NHS and welfare.

Welfare dissatisfaction

Yet gradually the agreement about and satisfaction with the welfare state weakened. There had always been two elements within it – health care and provision of social services – and it was the latter that came under attack. Some Conservatives in the 1960s became doubtful about the principle of universality (Fisher, 1973, pp. 270–1). They favoured selectivity in provision, as a means both of reducing the rising costs of welfare and of concentrating help on those most in need. Tory Party leaders were cautious, however, because talk of selectivity evoked memories of the hated stigma of the pre-war means test. On the Left the academic research by Titmuss, Townsend and Abel-Smith and the activities of poverty pressure groups like the Child Poverty Action Group showed that the welfare state had not succeeded in eliminating large-scale want: poverty was 'rediscovered'. Their reports were critical of Labour governments' records on welfare and equality between 1964 and 1970 and from 1974 to 1979.

The researchers were able to show that the welfare state and tax system were not necessarily redistributive from the rich to the poor. Some types of government spending and tax relief actually promoted inequality. For example state expenditure on higher education, subsidies for some commuter and inter-city train services, and tax relief on mortgages and private pensions, disproportionately benefited those from the middle class (Le Grand, 1982). The government-commissioned Black Report (1980) showed the persistent inequalities between social classes in health, and research by Halsey, Heath and Ridge (1979) did the same for education. The attacks on the welfare state from its natural supporters may have helped to undermine its legitimacy. After all, the revisionist wing of the Labour Party had stressed the importance of equality rather than public ownership as the goal of socialism (see p. 27). It argued that the task of a Labour government was to advance social and economic equality by reforms in taxation and education and by ever-growing expenditure on social welfare. Ever-increasing economic growth, it claimed, would enable equality to be reached painlessly – the cake could be both had and eaten – and in this way the egalitarian values of Social Democracy would be entrenched.

It was, however, it was the inability of the Labour Government to deliver sustained growth that led to a questioning not only of the Labour Right's economic analysis but also of the role of the welfare state. Economic growth in the 1950s and 1960s had eased distributional conflicts for funds between taxpayers and consumers of state services and between the different state services. Economic expansion provided what Richard Rose has called the three faces of affluence: growing public expenditure, growing national product and growing take-home pay (Rose and Peters, 1978). Between 1961 and 1975 public expenditure increased from 35 per cent to 45 per cent of GDP and spending on welfare grew from 18 per cent to 29 per cent of all public spending. Pressure for this increase came from the growing numbers of consumers of welfare and health services, as well as from producers of the services. But in the mid-1970s slower economic growth meant that greater welfare spending had to be financed out of higher taxes and/or increased charges. In 1960 the average taxpayer had paid about 8 per cent of income in tax and insurance contributions; by 1976 the proportion had increased to a quarter. From 1951 to 1975, public spending rose in constant terms in 23 of the 25 years.

Yet Britain was actually spending less as a proportion of GDP on health and welfare than many other Western states. One explanation was that other states were more successful in running their economies and were therefore able to provide more resources. Among the biggest spenders on welfare were Sweden, Norway and Denmark. It is true that for most of the post-war period these countries had governments of the Left. Perhaps more important was the fact that they were among the richest countries in the world. A second problem was the failure of some of Beveridge's assumptions. The growth of large scale unemployment from the mid-1970s and particularly after 1979 imposed a heavy burden on the social security bill. National assistance (now supplementary benefit) was no longer a safety net for the few as envisaged by Beveridge, but a system of provision for very large numbers. By the 1980s it was actually coping with demands from 5 million people, particularly the long-term unemployed or the very old, who had run out of contributions.

But the down-turn in economic growth was only one aspect of the so-called crisis. Supporters of claimants complained that too often the welfare state was an unresponsive bureaucracy that had become too complex. The liberal Right objected to it as a form of tax coercion.

Welfare and ideology

Not surprisingly, the debate about welfare sharpened. A number of Marxist and neo-Marxist writers claimed that the slow-down of economic growth was producing a new 'contradiction' in capitalism. They claimed that advanced capitalist societies required a high level of welfare spending to gain popular support, or compliance, as well as investment for further economic growth. The former, however, was increasingly being achieved at the cost of squeezing the profits of industry, and therefore causing an investment crisis. Hence the 'contradiction', or fiscal crisis, of the capitalist state, arising from the conflicting needs of maintaining political support and providing capital accumulation (O'Connor, 1973). Other radicals – some working in the social services – claimed that all that welfare did was to provide an inadequate bandage for the wounds inflicted on the poor by capitalism.

Ironically, the political Right also claimed that high levels of welfare spending were actually undermining the productive economy (Bacon and Eltis, 1976; see p. 45). High taxes, it claimed, weakened incentives to work harder. Universal benefits meant that welfare was spread too thinly and could not deal with the more serious cases of poverty. Some critics thought that there should be stiffer tests for eligibility for benefits or even increased use of pricing for some services (for example, health or education). They seized on the criticisms of the left that the services were not good enough and could be improved. But instead of making the case for more resources, the Right argued that if the services were not working well, then the approach should be changed. The increasingly dominant role in welfare played by the state weakened the values of individual self-reliance, family and community solidarity and private charity. Perhaps the welfare ethic, by removing the risks and disciplines of the market, undermined the work ethic.

An understanding of the political philosophy of Mrs Thatcher is crucial to explaining the attitude of the 1979 Conservative Government to the welfare state (Kavanagh, 1987). Mrs Thatcher is a self-made, first generation politician.

Such people, who have succeeded largely through their own intiatives, often find it difficult to understand why other people do not also succeed. If success and failure are largely the outcome of individual effort then perhaps 'failures' lack moral fibre or simply have not tried hard enough. Mrs Thatcher also believes that the market is the best means of promoting free choice and safeguarding personal liberty. This is a contrast to some other Conservative leaders who had been almost apologetic about the market. As far as possible people should solve their own problems or rely on their families and neighbours to help out. One should only turn to the state as a last resort. (Of course, Mrs Thatcher recognizes that the state has a vital role in maintaining the rule of law, public order, defence and stable money.) These values were expressed in the 1979 Conservative manifesto: 'We want to work with the grain of human nature, helping people to help themselves – and others. This is the way to restore that self-reliance and self-confidence which are the basis of personal responsibility and national success.' Nearly ten years later, on one memorable occasion in 1987, she claimed that there is no such entity as society, only individuals: 'And who is society? There is no such thing. There are individual men and women and there are families.'

She also sees herself as the defender of the taxpayer. The frequent cries for more spending on services are often, she claims, made by particular lobbies. Only the government can protect the hard-pressed taxpayers, many of whom may actually be poorer than the beneficiaries of particular programmes. Above all, she has distinguished herself from a number of her more upper-class Conservative colleagues by saying that she is not haunted by what she terms 'bourgeois guilt'. She does not feel that she has been responsible for the poverty and unemployment of the inter-war years – or of more recent times. Such an outlook is very different from that of Conservative leaders like Churchill, Macmillan and Butler who preceded her, and who were affected by such 'bourgeois guilt'. It is also very different from those Conservatives, such as Lord Whitelaw, who are sometimes called 'wet'.

But the 1979 Conservative Government's attitude to welfare rested on certain other assumptions. At a time of zero or low economic growth, improvements in services, and thus higher public spending, could only come from increased taxes. Yet a central plank of the government's economic policy was to reduce direct taxation and to restrain the growth of public spending. A cut-back or restraint on such spending was necessary both to fund tax cuts and to allow for the concentration of resources on the most needy. In 1979 Mrs Thatcher made election pledges to increase old age pensions in line with inflation and to protect the National Health Service. She made no commitments about other areas of welfare.

The Conservative record

The government, however, has found it difficult to rein back the growth in welfare expenditure. The increase in the number of people of pensionable age and, above all, the doubling in the numbers of unemployed between 1979 and 1982 placed a great strain upon social security spending. Much of this expenditure is demand-led – it is governed by the numbers of pensioners, unemployed, disabled and so on. Moreover, the level of many benefits is fixed by statute; for example, the annual uprating of pensions in line with rising prices. To date, the government has made some marginal changes in overall provision. In 1981 it cut the link between earnings and unemployment benefits and decided to uprate basic pensions and other benefits in line with price rather than wage increases (the latter of which were higher). The earnings-related supplements to benefits for the unemployed, the sick and widows, and to benefits for maternity and injury, were abolished. It also reduced the supplementary benefit entitlement for families of workers taking part in, or laid off by, strike action. More recently, it has frozen the value of child benefit allowances in 1987 and 1988.

Another example of the government's tinkering is seen in its attitude to the State Earnings Related Pensions scheme (SERPs). This was established by the Labour Government in 1975 with the support of the Conservative opposition. It became operational in 1978, although full earnings-related pensions were not due to come into effect until 1998. It was at last to provide reasonable pensions for those not in contracted-out occupational schemes, and remove the need for them to turn to supplementary benefit. SERPs would bring British pensions up to the levels paid at present in many other West European countries. SERPs is a pay-as-you-go scheme, with present contributions meeting the benefits for current pensions. The Conservative Government was worried about the dependency ratio – that is the number of people of working age per pensioner – which will steadily worsen in the second and third decades of the twenty-first century, and the pension commitment will be borne by a smaller number of taxpayers. In 1984 the Secretary of State for Social Services, Norman Fowler, mounted a review of various benefits including pensions. The report in December 1985 proposed to phase out SERPs by 1990. After much opposition the proposal was abandoned. In the end SERPs was scaled down and the proportion of earnings on which the final pension would be based was reduced from 25 per cent to 20 per cent. It was made easier for employers to contract out of occupational schemes and for individuals to opt for a 'portable pension', which they could transfer from job to job. Significantly, in spite of the encouragement of private pensions, the state will remain the major provider of pensions.

For most of its history the National Health Service has been the subject of a political consensus. The tenth, twentieth, thirtieth and fortieth anniversaries of the NHS were each marked by the governments of the day boasting of record numbers of patients treated, operations performed and doctors and nurses employed, and of growing levels of expenditure achieved during its term of office. Klein comments that the history of the NHS demonstrates the model of British party conflict as competition (in which the parties are 'rival salesmen') rather than confrontation (Klein, 1983). In general elections parties have competed about putting more resources into the service. In 1983 Mrs Thatcher claimed that the NHS was 'safe' with her and in 1987 she boasted of her government's increased spending on the NHS – in the previous eight years the Conservatives had 'spent more on the Health Service than any previous government', and the greater number of doctors, dentists and nurses were 'treating more patients than ever before in its history'. In its 1987 election manifesto Labour stated: 'Labour's proudest achievement is the achievement of the National Health Service.' It went on to promise a massive injection of funds, the phasing out of pay beds in the NHS and the 'reducing [of] prescription charges with the purpose of securing their eventual abolition'.

The consensus on the NHS thus remains firm in that hardly any political space exists for proposals which would seek to abolish free health care. Yet, if the principle behind the NHS remains intact, disagreement quickly emerged over how that principle should be made an organizational reality. Finance has always been a problem.

Pressure for resources

At one time it was thought by some (including Bevan) that demands on the service would decline as the health of the population improved. In fact, from the start, there has been a steady increase in expenditure. Among the pressures which have made for increased spending have been:

1 developments in medical technology and new forms of treatment, for example, in drugs, which means that a growing
   number of illnesses may be treated;
2 the pay pressures from 1.25 million workers in the service –
   their pay accounts for some 70 per cent of NHS expenditure;
3 the steady increase in the number of old people, who are
   particularly heavy users of the service. It has been calculated
   that real spending needs to increase by 1 per cent per annum
   simply to cope with the growing number of the very old.

Pressures for extra resources, and the political battles this gave rise to, have dogged the NHS. As Klein observes about health ministers, 'They could never do enough. The NHS was a machine for creating new demands' (1983, p. 40). Infinite demands faced finite resources. In 1949 the Labour Government took powers to impose prescription charges of one shilling (5 p). In 1951 Hugh Gaitskell's budget imposed charges for dental and ophthalmic treatment, prompting Bevan's resignation and a damaging bout of intra-party fighting. The issue has been highly sensitive ever since and Labour conferences have regularly called for the ending of such charges.

In 1951 and 1952 the Conservative Government considered proposals for ending free dental check-ups, discussed charges for stays in hospitals and then toyed with the idea of financing the NHS through national insurance contributions. On each occasion back-bench resistance or fear of electoral unpopularity turned ministers' thoughts away from such changes (Webster, 1988). The Labour Government abolished prescription charges on coming into office in 1964, only to be forced to reintroduce them in 1968 in an economic crisis. The decision to grant exemption to such categories as the old and the young, however, meant that 60 per cent of prescriptions were free and the yield was low. Critics, not necessarily all on the political Right, increasingly called for prescription and other charges to be raised as a means of providing extra funds, if the government would not find the money out of taxation.

Since the mid-1970s the NHS has become a more political issue. Like the rest of the welfare state it has encountered difficulties as governments have tried to restrain the growth of public spending. There have been pay pressures from increasingly militant producers – doctors, nurses and ancillary workers – who have been caught in government pay policies. In 1976 cash limits were imposed on the health service: the Treasury would make an allowance for pay and if this was exceeded (as it often was) then employers would have to draw funds from the rest of the health budget. Inevitably this meant a reduction in health service inputs and growing patient dissatisfaction.

In 1979 a Conservative government was elected, determined to squeeze public spending and pay in much of the public sector. Regular Treasury underfunding of pay awards forced authorities to make savings elsewhere in their budgets and to curtail services. There were growing complaints about the length of waiting lists for some operations, and reports of losses of key medical staff and of poor morale. The claims that the

NHS was starved of resources became increasingly topical in the 1980s and critics charged that the government hoped that dissatisfaction would encourage more patients to opt for private care. (Between 1979 and 1988 the number opting out doubled to 5.7 million.)

The government has made some changes since 1979. Prescription charges have increased more than ten-fold and in 1988, in spite of opposition in the party, free dental and eye check-ups were ended. Pay beds have been restored and health authorities have been encouraged to explore ways of raising funds. The government has also reintroduced tax relief for occupational health insurance for the relatively low paid. Management has become tougher in its pursuit of efficiency savings. At present a working group under Mrs Thatcher is reviewing the NHS. The fears and hopes of large scale privatization do not, according to signals, appear likely to be fulfilled. Conservative reformers are canvassing the possibilities of internal markets, which would allow patients to shop around different regional health authorities for operations, of providing tax relief for private medical insurance for the old, or even of introducing a special tax for health, with the resulting revenue going exclusively to that service. Yet the government seems wedded to the idea of the state playing the dominant role in health care.

For all the talk of the ending of the consensus on the National Health Service, continuity outweighs discontinuity. Reliance on taxation remains the overwhelming source of finance and the original structure and organization are largely intact. As Mrs Thatcher constantly points out, spending on the NHS between 1979 and 1987 increased by one third in real terms and there has been an impressive growth in the number of patients treated, substantial improvements in nurses' pay and a record number of hospitals built. In many respects, the inputs, measured in expenditure terms, have been more impressive than Labour's performance between 1974 and 1979.

Yet on the question of resources, it is worth noting that total private and public health spending, at less than 6 per cent of GNP, is markedly less than that in many Western states.

Britain spends a smaller proportion of national income on health care than all but four of the 20 member states of the Organization for Economic Cooperation and Development. (The four are Spain, Portugal, Greece and New Zealand.) The privately insured health system in the United States produces nearly twice as much spending (11 per cent) as a proportion of GNP. Although comparative figures suggest some underfunding in the UK it is difficult to argue that health care and services are, considered all round, twice as good in the US (indeed, on rates of infant mortality and life expectancy, they are worse). It has often been observed that central control of finance enhances the British Government's ability to ration resources and actually keep spending down. Far from being wasteful, 'nationalization' and central funding of the health service have probably proved more economical than a privately insured system.

The Labour Party certainly wishes to portray the NHS as a fundamental divide between the political parties; between the party of equality and public provision and the party of privatization and privilege. Labour objects to private health care on the grounds that something as important as health should not be affected by the patients' ability to pay, and it fears that private provision may lead to the emergence of a two-tier service in which the state service deals largely with those who are poor, are very old, or have illnesses that are intractable or extremely expensive to treat. Private insurance cover, it claims, will only deal with low risk categories. Its 1987 election manifesto declared: 'Labour will end privatization in the NHS, relieve the pressure on NHS facilities by beginning to phase out pay beds and remove public subsidies to private health.' The party continually refers to the inadequacies and inequalities of the United States' system of health care and claims that the Conservatives want to introduce something similar here. Conservatives, on the other hand, claim that people have already contributed through taxation to the NHS and that, in a free society, individuals should be able to spend their money as they choose. If people can spend their post-tax income on cigarettes and alcohol why cannot they invest in good health treatment? In the 1987 general election Mrs Thatcher boldly defended her own use of private health facilities, arguing: 'I want [to enter hospital] at the time I want and with the doctor I want . . . I exercise my right as a free citizen to spend my own money in my own way.'

Conclusion

Between 1979 and 1987 total real spending on social security grew by a third, with the major increases being in unemployment benefits, health and pensions. Elsewhere in the provision of social services, total real expenditure on education has remained stable but that on housing has been sharply reduced. The changes include symbolic measures (such as restoring pay beds in the NHS), cuts (usually for less popular targets such as housing benefit and supplementary and housing benefit in vacations for students), increased charges in council housing and health, encouragement of private medical insurance, rhetoric about reducing 'dependency' on the state, and some privatization of services (such as hospital catering and cleaning). Yet the role of the state in welfare provision remains dominant. Over 20 million people, or 89 per cent of families, are in receipt of benefits from the state, nearly half of them pensions (Rose, 1985, p. 369). To many the state is still 'Santa Claus'.

This is likely to remain the case until alternative or additional ways of financing social security programmes and the National Health Service are adopted. These are the two largest spending programmes of the government. Less than 10 per cent of children of school age are in the private sector and less than 10 per cent are covered by private health insurance. The government has also been aware that surveys suggest that since 1979 the public supports greater spending on welfare services even if this means increases in taxation, rather than tax cuts if this leads to cuts in welfare services. It is interesting that over time the rhetoric of those speaking for the government, particularly that of Mrs Thatcher, has changed to boasting of how much more staffing and money is devoted to the NHS and how much more is spent on the welfare state. According to opinion polls, however, the Conservatives run well behind Labour as the party best able to deal with the NHS as well as on other 'caring' social issues, like education and pensions.

Radical Thatcherism has reduced the independence and influence of the trade unions, nationalized industries, local government and civil service. In housing and education especially, the role of local government has been, or looks set to be, substantially reduced. The government defends its programme of selling council houses to tenants and allowing schools and other council house tenants to 'opt out' of local control as a means of promoting freedom and choice. To date, however, the elaborate system of state welfare and health care has resisted the Thatcherite tide; it remains so far the most solidly implanted of all the planks of the domestic post-war consensus.

6 Foreign and Defence Policy

In discussing the role of foreign and defence policy in the establishment and evolution of the post-war consensus, two preliminary points need to be kept in mind. One concerns the place of such policy within the political process, the other the role of recent history. Foreign policy, together with its agent, defence policy, form part of what Richard Rose (1976) terms the essential or defining functions of the state. Foreign policy is concerned with protecting the national community from possible attack by other communities, establishing and maintaining structures necessary for international economic activity, and developing the state's influence in relation to other states (Frankel, 1975). To the extent that foreign and defence policy thus concern themselves with the 'life-and-death' issues of national survival, it may be thought that there would always be a very strong agreement among political forces of all types about their shape.

In the case of Britain this is very largely true. With one exception there has been no time in recent history when a significant proportion of the political nation has refused to accept the state's definition of where the national interest lay. (The exception is of course Ireland; it is worth remembering that the United Kingdom was the only major Western combatant in the First World War to experience a nationalist uprising whilst the war was in progress.) Thus the phenomenon of large political movements standing outside and against the dominant definition of the national interest and its foreign policy expression has not existed in Britain. Anti-militarism has always been relatively weak and attempts at military sub-version unsuccessful. In this way the British political experience differs markedly from that of its nearest neighbour, France, where a powerful Communist Party was for a long period able to challenge the underlying premises of state foreign policy. For Frankel, British foreign policy has always been marked by pragmatism and an absence of ideology, qualities which can only exist when there is a high degree of political agreement about ultimate political purposes and national identity. He also notes that neither of the two major studies of the British party system – by Beer (1969) and by McKenzie (1955) – contain foreign policy in their index (Frankel, 1975, p. 32).

This is not to say, however, that the contents of foreign and defence policy have always been uncontroversial. The Boer War, the appeasement policy of the 1930s, the Suez Crisis of 1956 and Britain's relations with the European Economic Community have all provoked fierce domestic controversy. But such disagreement has generally been over a single issue – or a single set of issues – rather than over fundamentals. In the 1930s, for example, there was a wide gulf between the parties in Parliament on important questions like appeasement and the Spanish Civil War; and the official Labour opposition refused to vote for the military estimates. Yet the leader of the Labour Party, Attlee, was quite happy to sit on a Royal Commission investigating the future constitutional status of India and the party increasingly moved away from its pacifist traditions to a more robust acceptance of the need for strong armed forces. Moreover, it is also the case that foreign policy disagreements have often occurred *within* parties rather than between them and that they have been most effectively publicized by organizations that are independent of the major parties – the Union of Democratic Control in the First World War, the Peace Pledge Union in the 1930s and, more recently, the Campaign for Nuclear Disarmament and, perhaps, the League of Empire Loyalists.

The impact of the Second World War

The Second World War gave a tremendous boost to the forces within British politics that accepted a foreign policy consensus. There were, of course, disagreements – broad sections of left-wing opinion outside Parliament agitated for a Second Front to take the pressure off the Soviet Union and the only vote of censure the Coalition Government had to face came after the fall of Singapore in early 1942. But the war manifestly consolidated shared assumptions about the goals of foreign policy. (The contrast with wartime France is obvious.) Another consequence of the war was to strengthen the legitimacy of Labour as a party of government. While it is true that Labour ministers were largely active in the field of domestic policy, the fact that they were members of the War Cabinet, that Attlee deputized for Churchill in Britain when Churchill was abroad, and that Sir Stafford Cripps – a highly controversial Labour radical before 1939 – was sent as government representative both to the USSR and to India, helped to diminish any feeling that the interests of the nation would be unsafe in Labour's hands. Indeed, the poor record of the Conservatives in dealing with the dictators damaged what had traditionally been one of their strongest assets, namely their competence as guardians of British national interests abroad. Thus when Labour came to power in 1945 it was confident of its ability to manage the international as well as the domestic environment.

It is therefore not surprising that the elements of foreign and defence policy that were laid down in the following years should have proved to be so enduring. Atlanticism, the development of an independent nuclear deterrent, the process of imperial disengagement and reluctant Europeanism: all originated in the 1945 Labour Government and were subsequently continued, with little alteration, by its successors. Yet, ironically, the Labour Party first became a national party in the early 1920s out of its opposition to the existing policies and processes, which had created the slaughter of the First World War.

In 1945 there was much talk of a 'socialist foreign policy' which, for all its intellectual vapidity, did encompass themes that were largely absent from Tory thinking. The most important of these was the desire for harmonious and even friendly relations with the Soviet Union, whose prestige in 1945 was extremely high. It was argued that 'Left could talk to Left' in a way that Churchill – who had referred to the 'foul baboonery' of Bolshevism -never could. The obverse of this pro-Soviet stance was that many Labour politicians displayed what Morgan calls a Pavlovian anti-Americanism (Morgan, 1985, p. 272), a sentiment increased by US policy in the immediate post-war period – the summary abandonment of Lend Lease, the aggressive liberalism of its trade policy, the harsh terms attached to the 1946 loan and the failure to honour the 1943 Quebec agreement on the pooling of atomic information. Labour was committed in a way that Conservatives were not to racial equality, internationalism and 'the brotherhood of man', which meant enthusiastic acceptance of a multiracial, internationalist Commonwealth and also of the United Nations.

Reasons for the consensus

Thus the post-war consensus needs to be explained rather than simply assumed. A number of factors are relevant. The first concerns the perceptions Labour, and particularly its foreign secretary, Ernest Bevin, had of the international environment. The fact that Britain had been victorious in 1945 and had fought the war from beginning to end strengthened what might be called 'great power' confidence. The weakness of most West European countries – victors as well as vanquished – meant that Britain was by far the strongest military power in the region. The bounds of the British Empire were wider in 1945 than they had ever been; there was even a possibility that they might be extended to include the former Italian colonies. Relationships, diplomatic and commercial, with the Commonwealth were very close. British foreign policy therefore rested on the assumption that Britain was a world power. The natural consequence of this was that Britain needed the military resources of a world power – and that meant possession of an independent nuclear deterrent. In January 1947 the Labour Government decided to develop its own bomb. That this decision was taken in great secrecy without most of the Cabinet, let alone the parliamentary party, being informed says much about its political sensitivity. The important point, however, is that the Attlee Government's actions fitted into an assessment of Britain's role as a world power that majority opinion in both parties accepted. There was never any Conservative hostility to the possession of an independent deterrent or to Bevin's claim that the bomb must have a Union Jack on it. Sir Anthony Eden wrote of his agreement with Bevin and added, 'I would probably have agreed with him more, if I had not been anxious to embarrass him less' (1960, p. 5).

The second theme to emerge after 1945 was the recognition of the centrality of the United States to the defence of British and European interests. This was something that did not occur painlessly, either in Britain or, for that matter, in the United States which expected to withdraw all its troops from Europe soon after hostilities ended. As well as the irritation caused by US economic policies, there was much resentment at what was seen as US malevolence towards European colonial interests (notably the crescendo of press criticism of British policy in Palestine, and the support for Indonesian nationalists against the Dutch colonialists). Yet the dominant fact for European states soon became the apparent threat that the Soviet Union posed to their stability and in some cases to their existence. The Cold War came to dominate the international environment.

Britain was not menaced by large domestic Communist parties, as were France and Italy. Soviet intransigence in all the post-war negotiations between the members of the Wartime alliance, however, and its support for nationalist insurgency in the colonies, led Bevin to believe that the USSR did pose a threat to British security and that US support was vital to counteract it. The most famous expression of British attitudes towards the Soviet Union was Churchill's 'Iron Curtain' speech at Fulton, Missouri, in 1946. As foreign secretary of a Labour government Bevin was bound to criticize it publicly; but he had been fully briefed about it in advance and basically agreed with its contents. (Morgan, 1985, p. 245).

The breakdown of the wartime alliance with the USSR led to

the maintenance of high levels of defence expenditure and conscription. Britain's defence expenditure in 1952 was higher in *per capita* terms than that of the United States. Another consequence was the successful attempt to bind the USA to Western Europe by a formal military alliance in peacetime (a move, of course, to which the USA was traditionally hostile). The Atlantic Alliance was not something imposed upon an unwilling Europe by the State Department: it was, rather, the result of pressure from the Europeans and particularly from Britain. The signing of the treaty in 1949 was approved virtually unanimously in the House of Commons. Even 'Keep Left' Labour back-benchers (like Michael Foot), who had originally viewed United States influence with suspicion, were by the late 1940s convinced of the need for American support in the face of the Soviet threat, particularly in the wake of the destruction of socialist parties in Eastern Europe. The bulk of the Labour Party – and almost all Conservatives – viewed US military and economic assistance (the latter symbolized by Marshall Aid) with enthusiasm.

European integration

The third element in the foreign policy consensus was the attitude towards institutions of European integration. Political leaders in many West European states – France, Germany, Italy and the Benelux countries – became convinced by the experience of the Second World War that the only way to guarantee peace was to foster a supra-national culture that would draw the sting of nationalism. Nationalism came to be seen as a threat to, rather than the guarantor of, political and civil liberties; common European values needed common institutions if the challenge from the Soviet Union was to be contained; economic integration would not only benefit individual countries but create a trading bloc able to compete more equally with the American giant.

The more ambitious schemes of European federalists foundered on the rock of enduring national identities. But during the 1950s a number of initiatives were taken that put flesh on the ideal of Europeanism. The first of these was the formation of the Coal and Steel Community in 1950, which established a common market and supra-national control of iron and steel production for France, German Belgium, Italy, the Netherlands and Luxemburg. The second, which failed, was the proposal for a common defence force, the European Defence Community, in 1954. The third was the successful creation in 1957 of the common atomic programme, Euratom, and, above all, of the European Economic Community.

British governments of both parties refused to take part in any of these ventures. The so-called Schuman Plan of 1950 was viewed by the Labour Party with almost total hostility (Morgan, 1955, p. 419) and was rejected by the Cabinet on 25 June. Tory opinion was guardedly more favourable (largely on grounds of political tactics but also because of the misty sentimentalism of Churchill's European rhetoric). In government, however, the Conservatives did nothing to advance British participation in European institutions. The European Defence Community was out of the question and the prospect of membership of the EEC in 1957 attracted no real interest from the leaders of either party. Both parties agreed that Britain should maintain troops in Europe (a big change from earlier refusals of such permanent commitment) but neither saw Britain as a probable member of a supra-national organization. The famous phrase of Anthony Eden about European federation, 'We know in our bones that this is something we cannot do', applied in general to the attitude to Europe in the creation of the post-war foreign policy consensus. Significantly, in 1950 the strongest defence of the Schuman Plan for coal and steel integration was left to a back-bencher – Mr Heath.

Empire to commonwealth

The issue of Europe was one in which the politicians were able to impose their wills on permanent officials who, in some cases, were rather more enthusiastic about moves for integration. There was by contrast, a greater unity within Whitehall about the other major theme in British foreign policy, namely

Britain's future role in policing the world and as an imperial power. From the outset the Labour Government decided that the former role was impossible given Britain's economic weakness – in February 1947 British forces withdrew from Greece and in September of that year the Cabinet decided to withdraw troops from Palestine by August 1948. There was little serious opposition to these acknowledgements of the constraints on British power, apart from some predictable grumblings from Churchill about 'scuttle' or retreat.

But by far the greatest withdrawal – if that is the right word – came with the granting of independence to the Indian subcontinent in 1947. By 1950 independence had been granted not only to India, Pakistan and Burma, but also to Ceylon, Malta and Newfoundland. This raised the whole question of what was left of British imperialism and as such might have been thought to be a major area of partisan conflict. The ideological and emotional registers of the two parties differed widely. The Conservatives identified strongly with the British Empire, whereas Labour was anti-imperialist and committed to racial equality. Where Conservatives had strong personal and economic ties with the settler communities, Labour's links were with future nationalist leaders like Menon, Nkrumah and Banda (who had been a doctor in North Shields). Churchill's hostility to Indian independence and to its charismatic leader, Gandhi, were legendary whereas the generally impassive Attlee was, acording to Morgan, unusually committed and passionate about India's future (Morgan, 1985, p. 219). Labour opposed the Conservative 'imperial rhetoric' with the idealism of a multiracial Commonwealth.

Yet it is in the area of colonial policy that post-war bipartisanship was perhaps at its strongest and was most explicitly asserted. There was unquestionably much unhappiness in Conservative ranks about the granting of independence to the Indian sub-continent; but the party leadership made little attempt to prevent the inevitable. The principles of Labour's colonial policy, which concentrated on economic and social progress and a gradualist approach to self-government (the word 'independence' was rarely used), were not challenged by the Conservatives. That this should be so indicates one of the chief characteristics of consensus politics – the intent to which it reflects the influence of individuals. The Conservative spokesman on colonial affairs was Oliver Stanley, who had been colonial secretary during the war and took an extremely progressive attitude towards the subject. His relations with the Labour minister, Arthur Creech Jones, were good; but most importantly he was able to deflect opposition from within his own party (Goldsworthy, 1971, pp. 182–4). It is a measure of how close relations were between the two spokesmen that when, in 1951, the new Labour colonial secretary criticized the pre-war record of Conservatives in the empire, this was seen as a deliberate attack on the ethics of bipartisanship (Goldsworthy, pp. 204–10).

Change and continuity in the 1950s and 1960s

As in other areas, the positive consensus between the parties on foreign and defence policy started to break down in the mid-1950s. In 1952 Churchill said that on social services, foreign affairs and defence, nine tenths of the people agreed on what had been done and what would be done (Seldon, 1981, p. 35). Yet within a year, bipartisanship in colonial policy was coming under increasing strain as Labour reacted to what it considered excessive use of force by the Conservative Government, especially in British Guyana. The Suez Crisis in 1956, of course, produced a near total breakdown of communications between the two parties and divided the country to an extent unknown since before the war. By 1964 the Labour Party was pledged to a fundamental renegotiation of the nuclear deterrent policy which Macmillan's government had constructed in the early 1960s and which had as its centrepiece the purchase from the USA of the Polaris missile system. Labour also expressed strong reservations about moves towards the EEC that Macmillan had initiated in 1961.

This shift in attitude away from positive consensus owes much to forces at work within the Labour Party, pushing it in a more adversarial direction on foreign policy. The 1950s were an unhappy period for Labour, with bitter conflict between

Right and Left over the future direction of the party – and also . over competing personal ambitions. In this conflict, the idea of a socialist foreign policy re-emerged as did the ever latent anti-Americanism. The Left attacked German rearmament, United States neo-colonialism and the language of Cold War Atlanticism. Though the party leadership accepted the development of the H bomb and was able until 1960 to resist calls for unilateralism (calls which succeeded only for a year), its need not to cut itself off totally from its base inevitably led to a sharper tone in foreign policy debates. Gaitskell's negative reaction to the EEC, which so dismayed his Europeanist allies, owes much to this kind of party calculation.

Decolonization

Decolonization became one important theme of partisan conflict. In opposition Labour assumed a more moralistic tone towards Britain's colonial possessions and rejected the hitherto consensual appeal to gradualism in the process of achieving independence. In 1954, the Movement for Colonial Freedom was founded (with Anthony Wedgwood Benn as its treasurer). The MCF spoke of independence rather than self-government, attacked the economic exploitation motive in colonialism and denounced (via spokesmen like Woodrow Wyatt) the brutal tactics employed by British security forces in dealing with insurgency in Malaya and Kenya. Though officially non-party, the MCF was dominated by Labour and identified the Labour Party with the cause of colonial freedom. Kenneth Kaunda the future president of Zambia, would say in 1967 'We used almost to sleep by the radio each time there was a general election in Britain, praying and hoping that the Labour Party would be returned to power' (Goldsworthy, 1971, p. 358).

Yet what is most striking about the 1950s and 1960s is the underlying solidarity of the tenets of post-war settlement. As far as the colonies are concerned, movement came from the Conservatives, and it is remarkable how quickly the change occurred. On becoming prime minister in 1951, Churchill had announced that he had no intention of presiding over the dissolution of the

British Empire. Although Sudan (1955) and Ghana (1957) achieved independence and British troops were withdrawn from the Suez Canal zone in 1954, there was no clear philosophy of decolonialism, and the Suez Crisis of 1956 suggested a nostalgia for imperialism (a reason why the expedition was so unpopular in the United States). Conservative thinking assumed that an eventual orderly handover would require lengthy preparation and that this would in any case apply mainly to the indigenous colonies, where few whites lived. In both the so-called kith and kin colonies (notably the states of the Central African Federation with a large settler population) and the fortress colonies deemed vital for strategic reasons (Malta, Gibraltar, Aden, Suez, Hong Kong and Singapore), the process would be different. The Macmillan Government appeared committed to settler-dominated constitutional arrangements for the Central African Federation. In 1959 the Colonial Office was arguing that countries like Kenya and Uganda would not be ready for self-government before the 1970s.

A list of the colonies that gained independence within the next ten years gives an idea of the extent of the revolution that occurred. Between 1959 and 1964 independence came to the following British colonies: Cyprus, Nigeria, Sierra Leone, Tanganyika, Jamaica, Trinidad, Uganda, Singapore, North Borneo, Sarawak, Zanzibar, Kenya, Nyasaland and Malta. During the Labour Government's 1964–70 period of office, Northern Rhodesia, the Gambia, British Guiana, Bechuanaland, Basutoland, Barbados, the Leeward and Windward Islands, Aden, Mauritius and Swaziland also acquired full self-government (Goldsworthy, 1971, p. 36). The process of decolonization was, of course, a Europe-wide phenomenon that included the precipitate Belgian withdrawal from the Congo and the end of French Algeria; but nowhere did it occur with less domestic upheaval than in Britain.

The role of individuals was important in creating a consensus which the highly disciplined nature of party politics (particularly in the case of the Conservatives) made it possible to sustain. Macmillan confirmed an altered perspective with his famous 'Wind of Change' speech in South Africa in 1960. As colonial secretary between 1959 and 1961, Iain Macleod grasped the nettle of colonial independence and black majority rule. He initiated a series of constitutional conferences, over Kenya and Nyasaland, that would break the hopes of the white settler population with whom Conservative sentiment had strongly identified. It was a classic example of elite consensus overcoming partisan unease. In February 1961 Labour's spokesman on the colonies, James Callaghan, said in the House of Commons, 'I have not been conscious of any gulf [between himself and Macleod] over the last eighteen months' (Goldsworthy, p. 364). Five years later the Conservative leadership would anger many of its supporters by refusing to oppose the Wilson Government's imposition of sanctions on Southern Rhodesia.

Other areas

The same process of inter-party agreement can be seen in other areas of the consensus: Atlanticism, the independent nuclear deterrent and the withdrawal from a world role into Europe. The first two of these posed no problem at all to the Conservatives and became even more marked in the early 1960s. As prime minister, Macmillan was determined not only to repair the damage done to Anglo-American relations by the Suez Crisis but also to stifle attempts that were being made in Washington, particularly after Kennedy became president in 1961, to downgrade the importance of the 'special relationship' between Britain and the USA and to challenge the usefulness of Britain's independent deterrent. He succeeded in 1958 in obtaining amendments to the 1946 McMahon Act, which had prohibited foreigners' access to American nuclear secrets; and in 1957 introduced a seminal White Paper on Defence which announced the end of national service, a drastic cut in the number of troops and the establishment of the nuclear deterrent as the corner-stone of British defence policy (Frankel, 1975, p. 290; Pierre, 1972, p. 96).

The nuclearization of British defence policy occurred partly for reasons of economy, yet it quickly came up against the great constraint on Britain's foreign policy – the resource gap. It was after the abandonment in 1960 of a British missile system, Blue Streak, and the cancellation by the Americans of another one, Skybolt, that Macmillan obtained from the US president, in the Nassau Agreement of 1962, the right to purchase the submarine-based Polaris system. The closeness, if not dependency, that characterized Anglo-American relations in both defence and foreign policy was obvious. Indeed, the Conservatives' pro-Americanism was a major reason for de Gaulle's rejection of Britain's bid to enter the EEC in 1963 (see p. 105).

Thus Conservative support for the principles and institutions of Atlanticism was easy. For Labour the position was more complicated. We have already noted that a culture of anti-Americanism reasserted itself in the party after 1951. By 1960 it was also represented in the trade unions. The Campaign for Nuclear Disarmament (CND), inaugurated in February 1958, was supported by many Labour activists. Yet despite the increase in the size of left wing forces opposed to these central planks of the post-war settlement, official party policy remained, with one brief exception (see below), committed to them. For Labour leaders like Attlee, Gaitskell, Healey and Brown, Atlanticism posed no problem of conscience at all since they were all firmly committed to it. (So were the leaders of many European socialist parties, who had a strong aversion to the Soviet Union because of its destruction of social democracy in post-war Eastern Europe and its invasion of Hungary in 1956.) Gaitskell had threatened to resign from Attlee's Government if it did not support a UN resolution in 1951 that declared Communist China to be the aggressor in the Korean War. The major criticism of Suez was that it had damaged Anglo-American relations.

Things might have changed in 1963. Early in that year Harold Wilson, who had flirted with unilateralism, acquired the party leadership as the candidate of the Left. Two years earlier Gaitskell had made the rejection of the 1960 conference decision to withdraw from any alliance that relied on nuclear weapons a test of his leadership; in 1964 the Labour manifesto contained a pledge to renegotiate the Polaris agreement and raised the clear possibility of a non-nuclear future for Great Britain. In fact, Wilson's innate conformism soon asserted itself and both the deterrent and pro-Americanism remained the corner-stone of British foreign policy during his 1964–70 governments. Wilson was probably helped in his desire to preserve Atlanticism in the early years by the more attractive image of United States policy conveyed by Kennedy (with whom he strongly identified) and then by the Kennedy legend and the rhetoric of the 'great society'. Labour's official support for American policy in Vietnam brought great criticism from the British Left, both inside and outside the party, and played an important if background role in the breakdown of the consensus in the late 1970s and early 1980s (Neil Kinnock, for example, was a strong opponent of the Vietnam War in his student days). But this criticism left the government unmoved. The cancellation of a number of weapon projects and the 1968 decision to withdraw from most defence positions east of Suez marked a significant break with the past, but they owed much more to economic constraints than to any change in global strategy.

Shortly after he became prime minister, Wilson announced that Britain's frontiers were on the Himalayas, and he sought, like Macmillan, to play a world role as intermediary between Washington and Hanoi in the Vietnam conflict. Right at the end of his second premiership (1974–6) he authorized, in conditions of great secrecy, the updating of the Polaris system.

The attractions of Europe

It was in the 1960s that the leaderships of both parties came to believe that Britain could no longer play an independent role in world affairs and that the Commonwealth was not an adequate basis for protecting British interests. The withdrawal from the strategic bases east of Suez in the late 1960s (begun by Labour and completed under the Conservatives) was the culmination of a strategic retreat (Frankel, 1975, pp. 292, 300–2). The process whereby Britain came first to seek entry to, and ultimately join, the European Economic Community was a complicated one. It certainly did not produce high levels of inter-party agreement or anything approaching a national consensus. Indeed, in the early 1970s, Europe was one of the bitterest examples of the adversary style of politics which Professor Finer has described, and it subsequently played a major part in the breakup of the Labour Party in the early 1980s. Thus, to the extent that the EEC issue is an example of the consensus, it reinforces a point that has already been stressed – the elite nature of consensus politics and its divorce from party opinion.

In July 1961 the Macmillan Government decided to explore terms of entry into the European Economic Community. It is tempting to see this move as the European counterpart to the 'Wind of Change' speech referred to above. The decision to go for Europe, however, was not merely a response to decolonization – or even to the American statesman Dean Acheson's cruel and widely publicized remark about Britain's having lost an empire and not yet found a role. There was growing scepticism in Britain about the long-term prospects of the Commonwealth. It was no longer seen as a sufficiently dynamic trading area, particularly since many of its strongest members, like Canada and Australia, were manifestly uninterested in making Britain the hub of their economic activities. The sterling area's share of total British exports diminished from 48 per cent in 1950 to 30 per cent in 1960. Events such as the withdrawal of South Africa from the Commonwealth in 1961 and the first Commonwealth Immigration Act in 1962 further reduced confidence in its political value as a basis for British influence.

The questioning of the viability of the Commonwealth coincided with the sudden decline in confidence referred to elsewhere about Britain's prospects as a great power, both politically and economically. Within an extraordinarily short period of time the 'never had it so good' confidence of the 1959 election – in which EEC membership had not been an issue – was replaced by 'sick man of Europe' pessimism. Britain's overall economic performance was, rightly or wrongly, seen as faltering just when the six member countries of the EEC were bounding ahead. (The fact that French industrial production overtook Britain's for the first time since the nineteenth century was particularly wounding to national pride.) See table 6.1.

Table 6.1 Industrial production figures

Year (1953 = 100)	UK	The Six
1950	94	80
1958	114	144
1963	119	142

Source: Kitzinger, 1973, p. 29

The decision to approach Europe was in many ways based on calculations of political interest and influence; but it was the supposed commercial advantages that were most important. The decline in national confidence was the real wind of change in 1960 and it, rather than any long-maturing evolution in official thinking, led to the decision to approach the EEC. There was no popular pro-Europeanism and opinion in both parties was divided. The circumstances of the approach – a very poor balance of payments in 1960 leading to an austerity budget in 1961 – weakened the government's hand in its dealing with the EEC and gave de Gaulle the pretext, if not the reason, for his veto of the proposal in January 1963.

Europe provides a good example of how an issue, having once got on to the policy agenda, can become part of the consensus. In 1961–2 Labour adopted an increasingly hostile attitude towards the idea of Europe and, more especially, to the terms that the Macmillan Government sought to negotiate. To the surprise of many, the Labour leader, Gaitskell, showed considerable, almost contemptuous, scepticism about the EEC initiative. Though he did not reject the idea outright, he combined internationalist and nationalist rhetoric with a sharp sense of party advantage in condemning the 'Tory terms' which Macmillan was prepared to accept. He saw no reason to jeopardize a newly found party unity (the Left was very hostile to the EEC) or to allow the increasingly tired-looking Conservative government to drape itself in the robes of dynamic innovation. Wilson, Gaitskell's successor as party leader, was initially even more hostile to Europeanism. Yet in 1966 he too announced his interest in applying for EEC membership and in

March 1967 he applied. His reasons for doing so seem similar to those of Macmillan; the EEC was a potentially valuable solution to a period of economic and political difficulty.

In 1970 Mr Heath took over the application, which was still on the table, and committed the government to it more vigorously than his predecessor Mr Wilson had done. Mr Heath is perhaps the only true 'good European' to have been prime minister. Though he faced considerable opposition from within the Conservative Party in both Parliament and the country, his own determination, coupled with the greater resources of loyalty that a Tory leader is able to command, ensured that the negotiations were successful.

Yet in the passage of the European legislation, the role of the Labour Party was crucial. The party contained a great many anti-Europeans and in 1971 it voted to oppose the 'Tory terms' which Mr Heath had negotiated. The EEC became one of the main issues in a bitterly divided Parliament that showed few signs of a consensus on anything. With hindsight, however, it is clear that the Labour Party managers actually played an important enabling role in the processes whereby Britain finally joined the EEC. In 1971 many of those involved in the 1967 negotiations weakened the official Labour opposition by saying they would have accepted the terms arrived at by Mr Heath. The 1971 Labour conference voted against Tory terms but not against entry in principle, and in October of the same year 89 Labour MPs voted to approve the draft treaty without being deprived of the party whip. The following year when the bulk of the pro-European Labour MPs voted against the enabling legislation out of party discipline, a small number continued to support Heath, thus saving his government from defeat on more than one occasion (Kitzinger, 1973, p. 388). Perhaps the most decisive of Labour's acts in preserving the EEC was the 1975 referendum on whether Britain should stay in under the new terms which Wilson negotiated in 1974–5. The decision to hold a referendum was taken purely for reasons of internal party unity and owed nothing to any Europeanism or the desire to popularize a new constitutional mechanism. Yet the referendum gave a decisive endorsement to British membership: and the majority of the Labour

Cabinet, though not the party, threw its weight behind the 'yes vote'. There could hardly be a clearer example both of consensus and of the elite nature of consensus politics.

A limited breakdown

It is significant that in the volume *Ruling Performance* (Hennessy and Seldon, 1987), the chapters that deal with the governments of 1964–74 devote very little attention to foreign and defence policy. This is because the outlines of policy had really been established between 1959 and 1964 and neither party leadership dissented from the US-backed deterrent, withdrawal from Africa or Asia and belief in EEC membership. The significance of Europe, however, was that it showed that the foreign policy consensus depended primarily on a particular configuration of Labour leaders. It was the generation of 1945 – Wilson, Callaghan, Healey and Jenkins – who dominated foreign policy and kept it within the parameters laid down after the war. The withdrawal of key members of this group – first Wilson and then Callaghan and Jenkins – meant that Labour Party thinking on this, as on most matters, moved sharply away from the shared assumptions of the earlier period. The election of Michael Foot as party leader in 1980 brought to prominence one of the 1945 dissidents. Foot had never been an uncritical admirer of the Soviet Union and his fear of post-war Soviet expansionism in Eastern Europe led him to support the creation of the Atlantic Alliance. He was, however, a strong supporter of unilateral disarmament and was inclined right from the creation of CND in 1958 to see overseas conflicts in terms of a struggle between nationalist liberation and US neo-imperialism. He was also an unyielding opponent of British membership of the European Economic Community.

By the time of the 1983 election, the Labour Party was pledged to scrap the independent deterrent and pull out of the EEC. The latter was not perhaps a major political handicap, since Mrs Thatcher had, by her determination to cut Britain's contribution to Community funds, long deromanticized any feelings about Europe that public opinion may have had. But opposition to anti-Europeanism was probably the root –

though it was not the catalyst – of the split in the Labour Party that ultimately lead to the formation of the Social Democratic Party. And it is unquestionably the case that the unilateralist policy of Labour was, in its radicalism, a major break with the post-war consensus. It was also a considerable electoral disadvantage.

Not all elements of the post-war foreign policy consensus disintegrated with the arrival of both a radical opposition and a radical government, the latter led by someone with a deep suspicion of the consensual, if not actually compromising, style of the Foreign Office. Mrs Thatcher came to accept the broad parameters of conventional wisdom over black majority rule in Southern Rhodesia and Mr Foot never withdrew his initial support for the Falklands expedition. More recently, Mr Kinnock has removed British withdrawal from the EEC from the list of Labour policies. Though party disagreements over sanctions against South Africa are intense, they do no more than mirror the 1950s conflicts between supporters and opponents of immediate decolonization. Britain since the war has never known the sustained foreign policy conflicts that decolonization produced in France or that Vietnam caused in the United States.

Labour's uncompromisingly unilateralist posture made defence a central issue in politics and Mrs Thatcher's early foreign policy pronouncements, marked by their intense pro-Americanism and anti-Soviet rhetoric, grate against the 'honest broker' style of earlier governments. In general, however, a high level of consensus remains at both elite and popular level about the Atlantic Alliance. Membership of the EEC commands wide acceptance, if little enthusiasm, and the same is probably true of the Commonwealth. Indeed, British membership of such bodies as NATO, the European Community, the OECD and the seven member economic summit group, together with various other treaty commitments, impose constraints on what any government can do. Only the issue of nuclear arms fundamentally divides the parties from each other, having first divided Labour against itself, and here public opinion is largely behind the proponents of the old consensus.

Appendix: key dates in post-war foreign and defence policy

1947	British withdrawal from Indian subcontinent
1947	Decision to manufacture a British atomic bomb
1949	Britain joins the Atlantic Alliance
1954	Britain tests the H-bomb
1956	Suez Crisis
1957	Ghana achieves independence
1957	Defence White Paper adopts a nuclear-based defence strategy
1960	Start of large-scale decolonization process
1960	Last summit of superpowers which Britain attends automatically
1961	Macmillan Government applies for membership of the EEC
1967	Wilson Government applies to join EEC
1968	Wilson Government decides to withdraw British troops from East of Suez
1972	Health Government successfully concludes EEC negotiations
1974–9	Labour Government updates Polaris system
1980	Conservative Government decides to purchase Trident missile system
1981–2	Labour Party votes to abandon Polaris and remove American bases from Britain
1982	Britain recaptures Falkland islands from Argentina

7 Assessment

The preceding chapters have analysed the post-war consensus in terms of a range of parameters within which public policy decisions were taken. We have sought to show, firstly, that in this period it is continuity rather than discontinuity that characterizes the content of significant areas of public policy and, secondly, that such continuity existed alongside a highly adversarial party system. In no sense was post-war Britain a country without politics or without disagreement; our argument is that political disagreement took place within a broad set of shared assumptions about the goals – and the mechanisms – of government action. As Samuel Beer said, the Labour–Conservative battle throughout the 1950s and 1960s dealt with questions of 'more' or 'less' at a time when party differences were 'marginal', statistical, quantitative (Beer, 1969, p. 242).

Of course, there were significant social and economic changes in the years from 1945 to 1987. The level of unemployment at the time of the 1945 election was 112,000, at the 1987 election nearly 3 million. Home ownership soared from 26 per cent to over 66 per cent of all households. Real income more than doubled. The proportion of the workforce employed in manual work fell from over two thirds to less than a third. Britain was relegated from great power status to the second division in international affairs. Yet, perhaps surprisingly, the main features of the political system display remarkable persistence.

In this final chapter we will briefly summarize the policy

areas that together helped to create the consensus, before considering the range of factors that contributed to its breakdown and replacement after 1979 by the policies and values that are today associated with Thatcherism.

On *foreign policy and defence* the main policy lines had been established by 1950 and were largely matters of agreement thereafter. Membership of the Atlantic Alliance and a progressive withdrawal from Empire provoked little disagreement between the party leaderships. Although the Labour Party conference voted in 1960 against any defence policy based on the use of strategic nuclear weapons, and thus implicitly questioned British membership of NATO, the party leadership refused to accept this resolution and managed to have it reversed the following year. In the 1964 election Labour's pledge to renegotiate the Nassau agreement, which provided the Polaris submarine, appeared to commit it to phase out the independent nuclear deterrent; but this proved, as the party leadership had perhaps intended, to be no more than a smokescreen for a policy of maintaining it (Pierre, 1972, pp. 267–71). Membership of the European Community was actively pursued by all Governments after 1959, with the exception of the first Wilson Government of 1964–6. Each party faced dissent from within its ranks over these policy choices. The Conservative Right opposed the retreat from empire and the Labour Left opposed the British bomb. British membership of the Community was opposed by both groups and became one of the clearest cases of adversary politics in the 1960s and 1980s. When Labour was in opposition, it resisted Conservative attempts to enter the EEC, rejected the terms which were ultimately agreed in 1972 and demanded withdrawal between 1980 and 1983. Yet when in office the Labour leadership initiated an application to join in 1967 and then, in 1975, backed the referendum proposal that Britain should stay in the Community.

The role of the trade unions relates to two important policy areas (incomes restraint and industrial relations) and to the style of government decision-making. Some form of restraint in wage bargaining was always implicit in the commitment to full employment that government first accepted in 1944. The perceived capacity of organized labour to produce an unacceptable level of inflation if it pushed its bargaining power to the limit meant that an unfettered commitment to free collective bargaining was never really part of the post-war consensus. Apart from the Churchill and Eden administrations of 1951–7, all governments before Mrs Thatcher's experimented with some type of formal incomes policy. The history of incomes policy, like that of the EEC, is a classic case of adversary politics. Oppositions condemned the incomes policy of the government of the day but, when in power, introduced their own, usually as an emergency measure which they then sought to make into a permanent feature of national economic management. Incomes policies were politically damaging to governments. Mr Heath's defeat in 1974 appeared to mark the end of statutory income policy just as the fall of the Callaghan Government in 1979 led to the abandonment of the voluntary approach symbolized by the Social Contract. Henceforth the Thatcher Government would rely on control of the money supply and a high exchange rate, rather than incomes policy, to moderate inflation.

As far as industrial relations are concerned, the consensus divides into two periods. Before the mid 1960s, governments did not attempt to use the law to define and control industrial relations practices; afterwards they did. It was hoped that the law would inject greater discipline into industrial relations and strengthen official union leaders against shop floor power. The trade unions resisted, clinging to the voluntarist tradition, and only after 1979 did legislation begin to have an impact. Industrial relations legislation again illustrates adversary politics. The 1974 Labour Government scrapped much of the Tory 1971 Industrial Relations Act, and the Thatcher Government subsequently reversed some of Labour's legislation. At present Labour is also pledged to reverse the Thatcher laws on picketing.

For most of the post-war period the trade unions were consulted, almost as an estate of the realm. Both Mr Heath and Mr Wilson in the 1974 elections offered different versions of social contracts with the unions in which consultation on government social and economic policies would be traded for wage moderation. Since 1979 the unions' right to bargain with employers remains largely intact – though the balance has shifted in favour of the latter – but the government does not recognize the unions' quasi-political role. They are now rarely consulted. Thus since 1979 the change from the post-war period has been threefold; no incomes policy, no consultation, and the use of law.

On the *mixed economy* the continuity of policy between 1951 and 1979 was impressive. There was some limited rolling back of state ownership by the 1951 Conservative Government and some minor extension by the 1974 Labour Government. But these produced only marginal changes in the boundaries between the state and the private sectors. Since 1979, however, there has been a major programme of privatization. Across the industrial sector and the nation's housing stock the boundaries between private and public have been radically redrawn, a change due entirely to the policies of the Conservative Government.

Full employment was a continuous policy goal until the mid-1970s and is perhaps the dominant theme in the post-war political settlement. In 1950 the Conservative manifesto stated: 'We regard the maintenance of full employment as the first aim of a Conservative government', and that pledge remained a fundamental article of both parties' creeds. From the early 1960s, Conservative and Labour governments introduced a series of micro-economic measures to try to improve overall economic performance and preserve full employment. Incomes policies, planning, industrial relations reform and entry to the European Community represented a shift from the demand management methods of the 1950s to supply side measures. But the aim of full employment remained unchanged. It was circumstances – poor balance of payments leading to problems with sterling – rather than ideology that led to a decline in confidence about the possibility of demand management. The political elite came to acknowledge that traditional Keynesian methods of boosting purchasing power had unacceptable side effects; at each stage of the cycle, pump priming was producing fewer additional jobs at higher levels of inflation and undermining the currency. The formal turning-points are Mr

Healey's 1976 budget, which did not provide for full employment, and Mr Callaghan's speech to the Labour Party conference the same year (see p. 42). Since 1979, the Thatcher Government has explicitly stated that it is not the job of government to provide full employment; rather, it is achieved by responsible wage bargaining and firms providing goods of the right quality and at prices which people will pay.

On *welfare* there have been some significant trimmings in the provision of central benefits – notably in unemployment, sickness, supplementary and child benefits – but the broad picture remains essentially unaltered. Indeed, government spending on social security has increased in real terms by 40 per cent since 1979, largely because of the growth of unemployment. What politicians call the social wage remains as large as ever as a component of public spending. Yet it is also true that the underlying assumptions of the welfare state – flat-rate benefits, universal provision, and equality of access to and treatment in health care – are under greater questioning today. This is due in part to the Thatcher Government's policy of restraint on public spending and in part to the government's support for market rather than state provision. Ministers have encouraged the belief that the public should not look to government for a solution to many social problems.

Three observations can be made about this set of policies. The first is that up until 1970 governments tended to accept their predecessors' policies and legislation whereas after 1970 they rejected them, at least at the outset. Under Mr Heath in 1970 there were discontinuities on industrial and incomes policies; under Mr Wilson in 1974 new changes occurred in these two areas together with education and housing finance. Yet within a short period both the Heath and Wilson Governments made major U-turns on economic policy. The second point is the lack of fundamental institutional disagreements, comparable with the question of Irish Home Rule or reform of the House of Lords before 1914. Issues like public ownership and, more importantly, the European Community and devolution provoked some disagreement between parties and rather more within them. Yet the issues were widely regarded as being amenable to bargaining and both the EEC and devolution were actually resolved by referenda, a mechanism whereby the parties could lessen their own responsibility for policy.

The third feature of the 'policy set' is the continuing relevance of so many of its themes, 40 years after they first emerged. Issues such as the problem of high public spending, the cost of the NHS, the boundaries between the public and private sectors, the relationship of Britain and Europe, and the difficulty of reconciling free collective bargaining with stable prices and full employment, remain on the agenda of political debate, as they have done since the war. Within the parties, Labour's divisions over defence and nationalization remain, as do, albeit in a more muted form, Conservative disagreements about the proper role of government in managing society.

Breakup

It is possible to argue that the breakup of the consensus came much earlier than 1979. In the mid-1950s a generational change occurred in which the major figures of wartime and immediate post-war politics – Churchill, Eden, Attlee, Morrison – left the centre stage. New leaders like Gaitskell, Wilson and Heath injected a more adversarial tone into political debate. The 1950s were described at the time as witnessing the end of ideology, partly because of the apparent exhaustion of the late nineteenth-century 'world views' like Marxism and liberalism, and partly because of the apparent ability of managed – or welfare – capitalism to resolve the problems of industrial society. By contrast the late 1960s saw the emergence of a new radicalism both on the Left and the Right. At the time Mr Heath's free market policies seemed a sharp break with the past, and analysis of the party manifestoes also suggests that the ideological divide between the parties became sharper (Budge et al., 1987; Frankel, 1975). In February 1974 the parties were divided on incomes policy, EEC membership, the scale of public ownership and industrial relations.

It was only after 1979, however, that the breakup of the old consensus became apparent, as a result of the sheer scale of change that has occurred since Mrs Thatcher became prime minister. Only membership of the Atlantic Alliance, and (now) of the EEC, and commitment to the National Health Service remain from the old consensus. Indeed, it can be argued that, should Kenneth Baker's educational reforms be achieved, the NHS will be the only strand remaining from the 1945–50 domestic policy package. Most of the other planks – a large public sector, the commitment to full employment, acknowledgement of trade unionism's special role – have disappeared or at least been severely eroded. In defence matters Labour remains committed to abandoning the independent nuclear deterrent.

Explanations for the change

The fact that so many elements of the post-war consensus no longer hold needs to be explained as well as described. In seeking to understand the changes that have occurred in the governing assumptions and expectations referred to in chapter 1, we need to look at three variables: ideas, circumstances and individuals. In each of the policy areas referred to in this book, ideas and texts, socio-economic contexts and the beliefs and ambitions of individual political personalities came together to produce change. Thus it is the interaction of the three factors that is crucial.

Ideas

Very often in politics, a changing political opinion is signalled by the absorption by Government of ideas and policies advocated by the opposition. By 1950, for example, the Labour Government had abandoned economic planning and was relinquishing many controls over the economy. After 1959 the Macmillan Government turned to economic planning and incomes policies. By 1972 the Heath Government, in spite of its original philosophy of disengaging from industrial intervention and encouraging market forces, was seeking cooperation on an incomes policy with the unions and was intervening on a large scale in the economy.

It is striking how many of the values and policies subsequently associated with Thatcherism had already been accepted by key figures in the Labour Government. Monetarism, or the setting of monetary targets, had been introduced by the Labour chancellor Denis Healey in 1976. The same year saw the imposition of cash limits on many government programmes, a reduction in public spending plans, and a measure of privatization in the government's sale of part of British Petroleum. Mr Callaghan's Policy Unit drew up a scheme for the sale of council houses to tenants and was encouraging the prime minister to campaign on educational standards. Labour had already abandoned the commitment to Keynesianism and full employment. As Mr Callaghan told the 1976 party conference, Britain could no longer spend its way out of recession; this would only lead to 'high inflation followed by higher unemployment'. There was also general disillusion among Labour ministers about the benefits of higher public spending – often there was no discernible improvement in outputs, notably in educational standards (J. Barnett, 1982). It was a Labour minister, Anthony Crosland, who coined the phrase 'the party's over' to describe the end of ever more generous levels of government expenditure. Moreover, there were fears of an electoral backlash among skilled workers against the increased burden of taxation. If a significant feature of the postwar consensus was the degree to which many of the Labour ideas had already been absorbed by the Conservatives by 1950, something similar can be said about the Thatcherite ideas being absorbed by the Labour Government.

The legitimacy of new ideas did not, however, occur spontaneously, whether concerned with privatization, contracting out services, tax cuts, council house sales or trade union reform. The rediscovery of the virtues of market forces owed much to the work of a series of think tanks, most notably the Centre for Policy Studies (formed in 1974) and the Institute of Economic Affairs (formed in 1957). The latter aimed to influence the climate of opinion and drew on the free market and individualist writings of Hayek and Milton Friedman. Particularly important after 1974 were the speeches and writings of Sir Keith Joseph, whose influence derived in part from his closeness to Mrs Thatcher. These groups and Sir Keith thought that

Britain had taken a wrong turning in 1945. They explicitly sought to overturn the intellectual assumption – promises of full employment, state-provided universal welfare, state ownership, and pursuit of redistribution – of the Attlee consensus. The ideas of the New Right have been discussed earlier (see p. 44). In a word, it held that government was 'overloaded' and should do less.

Circumstances

Ideas and opinions do not exist in a vacuum; to have an impact they must relate to the concerns of policy-makers (see Pliatzky, 1984; J. Barnett, 1982). The breakup of the old consensus was in large measure due to the fact that it clearly was not working. Apparent abuses of trade union power became more flagrant after the disruption of the 1970s, and the antisocial activities of some trade unionists in the Winter of Discontent discredited the claim that the public sector necessarily provided public service. By overreaching themselves the unions helped to bring about the election of a Conservative Government and gave an opening to Mrs Thatcher's legislation. Keynesianism in the 1970s appeared to have no answer to stagflation. By 1974–5 the economy simultaneously suffered its worst balance of payments, record high unemployment and high inflation. The Winter of Discontent showed that it was well nigh impossible to work out long-term programmes of anti-inflation policies with the trade unions. At the same time pressures from the international financial markets (reflected in the selling of sterling) and the intervention of the IMF in 1976 also dictated a new range of policies and a concentrated effort to lower inflation. In other words, Mrs Thatcher was not preaching in the desert.

In many other Western democracies the economic recession, partly caused by rising prices of oil and other commodities, caused problems for public policy. The end of the long post-war boom created difficulties for Keynesianism. In a number of countries tax cuts, privatization and public spending constraints became the new policy watchwords (Cameron, 1983). Even left-wing administrations in Australia, New Zealand,

Spain and France had to change direction sharply. Yet it was in Britain that relative economic decline and apparent crises both of governability and social cohesion seemed most apparent. Domestic commentators (and also an American president, Gerald Ford) spoke in terms of a near-terminal 'British disease'.

Political personality

Changes in elite ideas and public opinion and the 'lessons' of events are not spontaneously transformed into political outputs. At the end of the day they have to be translated into policy decisions by human beings. The macro-factors of culture, economic trends and international forces have to be connected to the micro-factors of the calculations and actions – or non-actions – of individual politicians and other policy-makers. The roles of Margaret Thatcher, Sir Keith Joseph and Tony Benn are an important part of the story.

Much of the responsibility for breaking the consensus may be claimed by Mrs Thatcher (Kavanagh, 1987). She is the first post-war leader not to try to maintain the consensus. In 1981 she dismissed consensus as 'the process of abandoning all beliefs, principles, values and policies ... avoiding the very issues that have got to be solved merely to get people to come to an agreement on the way ahead'. Politicians were looking for new ways of combating inflation, curbing union power, encouraging economic market forces and restoring the authority of central government. Policy-makers turned to tax cuts, monetary targets, cash limits and the withdrawal from hitherto sacrosanct policy commitments (such as full employment levels).

Many of the radical policies – restrictions on the trade unions, prohibition of union membership for workers at GCHQ, rejection of social contracts or incomes policies, income tax cuts and privatization, as well as hostility to the civil service and local government and the imposition of the community charge – owe much to Mrs Thatcher's vigorous support. This is not the place to address the subject of prime ministerial power. Mrs Thatcher has chaired Cabinets in which ministers sharing her outlook have often been in a minority and she has lost a number of Cabinet battles. But she has won the great majority. We would argue that she does illustrate the formidable power a prime minister possesses – when the incumbent is determined, has a clear sense of purpose and effective strategy for realizing it, and is regarded as successful (be it in general elections, the Falklands, conflict with Arthur Scargill, or compared with Labour leaders). She has also weakened or removed some of the obstacles in her way by, for example, abolishing or financially confining left-wing local authorities, and weeding out or bypassing senior civil servants who are sceptical about her solutions and her methods. (Some commentators have complained that her close involvement in the promotion of civil servants has given the impression of politicization of the service.) Mrs Thatcher is not the explanation of all that has happened but she has made a difference, and a significant one.

Mrs Thatcher has also been lucky. She was lucky that Mr Callaghan did not dissolve Parliament, as he was widely expected to do, in the autumn of 1978. The Winter of Discontent then occurred, destroyed the credibility of the Labour Government and its much-vaunted relationship with the unions, and seemed to vindicate much of Mrs Thatcher's message. She has also been helped by divisions within the Labour Party and by the split in electoral support for the major non-Conservative parties. The electoral system has endowed her with parliamentary landslides, even with only 42 per cent or 43 per cent of the vote.

Meanwhile the Labour Party reacted to loss of office in 1970 and again in 1979 by shifting sharply to the left. *Labour's Programme 1973* doubted that reform of capitalism was possible: 'it cannot achieve any fundamental changes in the power relationships which dominate our society.' In 1980 the party elected Michael Foot as leader – regarded by most voters as a highly implausible possible prime minister. Inspired by Tony Benn the party changed its constitution to give greater power to the (predominantly left-wing) constituency activists and the unions in choosing the party leader and nominating parliamentary candidates. At the same time Labour's policy profile became much more radical, with commitments to unilateralism and withdrawal from the EEC and support for a whole range of minority interests. In 1981 a number of right-wingers left the party and formed the Social Democratic Party. Labour, according to surveys, appeared more divided and 'extreme' than ever. One commentator noted that Tony Benn captured the party and lost the country. To date, the party has still not recovered the ground lost between 1981 and 1982. Though the Liberal–SDP Alliance rose for a time in the political vacuum that resulted from Labour's problems, Mrs Thatcher has been its principal beneficiary.

In both Labour and Conservative Parties, internal forces mobilized in the 1970s to discredit the established leaders – Mr Heath for his record of electoral losses and the failure of his anti-inflation and industrial relations policies, and the Labour Right for its poor record of managing the economy after 1964 and after 1974. Electoral failure opened the way for opponents of the consensus to climb to the leadership of the Conservatives after 1974 and of Labour after 1979. Mr Benn and Labour's Left agreed with Sir Keith Joseph and Mrs Thatcher: the consensus had failed. Yet in 1979 the electorate was in many ways consensual – behind Conservative policies. Many Labour voters agreed with the great majority of Conservatives in supporting the sale of council houses to tenants, mandatory pre-strike ballots, encouraging private medicine, stopping payments to strikers' families and a halt to more nationalization (Rose, 1984).

The public mood

Vernon Bogdanor (1983) has suggested that the main threat to the post-war consensus was always thought to be from the Left – the Bevanites in the 1950s and Bennites in the 1970s – rather than from the Right. Supporters of the free market economy were regarded as eccentric: 'What could not have been so easily predicted was that it would be the Right, and not the Left, which would become the beneficiary of the collapse of the post-war settlement, Socialism rather than Conservatism which would be defeated by the slump.' The question then becomes that of trying to assess how much the post-1979 policies have created a new political settlement. Is there a 'new consensus'?

Mrs Thatcher has often claimed that changing the economy was only a means to the end of changing collectivist attitudes. The British Social Attitudes surveys suggest that Mrs Thatcher has failed to capture the hearts and minds of the British people (1988). The surveys find majorities favouring government provision of health care and a decent standard of living for the old and accepting that the trade unions have a legitimate role to play (Heath et al., 1985). Yet these may be rather poor measures of so-called 'Thatcherism'. Although tax cutting is a crucial part of the Thatcherite plans to increase self-reliance and roll back the state, surveys show that large majorities would prefer more state spending on health and education rather than cuts in income tax. But when voters are asked whether tax cuts or more public spending are better *for themselves and their families*, more are prepared to opt for the tax cuts. Calculations about interests are perhaps better predictors of voting behaviour than are the responses on more general issue questions.

The evidence about the public mood is ambiguous: people still seem attached to the welfare state and to the values it expresses, but welcome the Thatcher government's emphasis on incentives and enterprise. Although public opinion seems to have shifted to the right before 1979 – on tackling the power of the unions, public ownership and state spending versus tax cuts – it has not moved much since. The mood is complex and runs across the old Left-Right divide. There is widespread support for the free market as a means of wealth creation and for many of the policies this entails. The disappointing economic record of the 1970s may have helped the government by lowering popular expectations of what any government could do, notably in tackling unemployment. Surveys showed that voters are also prepared to blame the world recession and trade unions for the loss of jobs. But there is little evidence of any decline in popular commitment to the principles of collective, state funded provision of welfare. Research by Robert Worcester (1988) finds that the majority of Conservatives believe an ideal society would be characterized by an emphasis on caring for others rather than wealth creation. At the same time the ideal society of a third of Labour Party supporters is one that would increase efficiency at the expense of jobs and one that allows people to make and keep as much of their earnings as they can. It may be that Thatcherism so far has been half successful, repudiating Keynes but not Beveridge (Kavanagh, 1987).

What follows?

If Mrs Thatcher has helped to destroy major parts of the post-war consensus (it was already crumbling by 1979), the problem remains of whether she has established a new settlement. An answer to this will only become clear over time, either when there has been a successor non-Conservative government and one is able to see how much of what the recent governments have done is accepted, or if further Conservative governments carry on in the present spirit. There was a major division between the parties in the 1983 election. Labour promised that it would bring Britain out of the EEC in the lifetime of the Parliament, would abandon nuclear weapons and take back into public ownership assets which had been privatized. The party also promised to end compulsory council house sales and to allow councils to repurchase those which had been sold. It was difficult to envisage many Labour MPs (let alone activists) preferring lower taxes over higher benefits, more scope for the market and competition over regulation and intervention, and the profitable private commercial and industrial sector over nationalized industries. After 1983, however, Labour abandoned its opposition to British membership of the European Community, council house sales and pre-strike ballots. Before the 1987 election Mrs Thatcher spoke of wanting another term of office so that she could 'kill off socialism'. By this she seems to have meant less the elimination of the Labour Party (socialist or Labour parties exist as one of the two or three largest parties in every Western state except the United States and Ireland) than the curbing of its anti-capitalist, pro-state ownership orientations.

It is already difficult to see a future Labour government attempting to revert to the *status quo ante* on public ownership, taxation and industrial relations. Indeed, the present Conservative Government has announced plans to privatize water, electricity and steel and bring in further trade union legislation. A future Labour government will therefore start much further back from where it was in 1979, in terms of instruments to steer society and the economy. There are now, for example, no foreign exchange or prices and incomes controls, and the institutional supports for Labour in the trade unions, local government, council housing and nationalized industries have all been significantly eroded. Since 1979 there have also been significant social changes in the British electorate. Between 1979 and 1987 membership of unions fell from 30 per cent to 23 per cent; owner-occupation spread from 52 per cent to 62 per cent of homes; share-ownership increased from 7 per cent to 19 per cent, and middle-class households rose from 35 per cent to 42 per cent (MORI). Many of these changes have been assisted by Conservative policies and legislation. On balance they strengthen the electoral base of the Conservative Party and weaken that of Labour.

The Conservatives do seem to have uncovered a constituency since 1979 which has an interest in maintaining a government that pursues Thatcherite policies. It includes much of the affluent south, home owners, share owners and most of those in work, whose standard of living measured in post-tax incomes has improved steadily in recent years. In 1987 the Conservative Party gained just over half (55 per cent) of the middle-class vote. Nearly two thirds of the middle class working in the private sector voted Conservative, while only 44 per cent of those in the public sector did so. Among the working class it gained 36 per cent of the vote, its largest share in any post-war general election. This support was heavily concentrated on manual workers who were living in the south, were home owners, were private sector employees and those were not members of trade unions. This is what has been called the new working class; it is the more affluent, more 'privatized' and growing part. This section of the working class and the private sector middle class add up to a formidable electoral coalition for the Conservative Party at a time of three party politics.

Parties out of office for a long time do not, of course, come back with a clean slate. Much of the agenda and many existing spending and policy commitments will have been shaped by previous incumbents. In the United States, the Republicans in the 1950s had to come to terms with the Democrats' New Deal (which entailed a more active role for the federal government in the economy, help for the poor and acceptance of the USA's greater role in world affairs). In Sweden any non-socialist government has to operate within parameters established by the Social Democratic Party's hegemony in that country over the past 50 years. When the French Socialists returned to power in 1981 after 23 years in opposition they too had to accept a constitutional settlement which they had long con- demned. The Conservatives in 1951 had to come to terms with the legacy of the post-war Labour Government (particularly public ownership, the welfare state and the high public spend- ing these entailed). In the mid-1970s Sir Keith Joseph com- plained that previous Conservative governments had mistakenly pursued a middle ground, a point midway between Labour and Tory policies. But as each Labour Government moved further to the left, a move accommodated by subsequent Conservative administrations, so the middle ground moved to the left. Joseph called this the ratchet effect. Mrs Thatcher has reversed the ratchet and Labour almost certainly will have to move to the right in comparison with their position in 1979–80.

The impact of politics

One last question emerges from the record of government since 1979, and it concerns the role of parties in the British system. Do parties make a difference? It is interesting that in recent years critics of adversary politics have attacked the effects of the two-party system and the first-past-the-post electoral system. They have argued that because a party in opposition needs to distinguish itself from the government this, firstly, produces artificial divisions between the political parties and, secondly, ensures that when the opposition becomes the government it starts out with policies which have been drawn up in very different and highly partisan circumstances. Hence governments have been gradually 'educated' by events to produce U-turns in their policies. This happened with the Wilson Government by 1967, the Heath Government by 1972, and the Wilson/Callaghan Governments by 1976.

One should note that this is a very different assessment from the traditional view of the two-party system in Britain as the jewel in the crown of the political order. Defenders of the party system said that it provided choice for the voters and coherent and responsible programmes because of the likelihood that either party could form the government. In addition, since the parties were evenly matched in electoral support, there was some convergence in policies. Yet in the 1970s the critics of adversary politics (Finer, 1975) argued that political parties had too much, and too partisan, an impact. They claimed that the system produced damaging reversals and discontinuities in policy.

Proponents of the view that parties should have a significant impact on policy argue that, as a popularly elected body, government is sovereign. They may also claim that failures of government to carry out their policy intentions are a devaluation of the electoral process. On the other hand, democracy also allows for checks and balances on the elected government and for decisions to be made by bodies other than central government. Perhaps parties should not make too much difference in a society such as Britain's which purports to be consensual and which, in comparative terms, still is. The view of Richard Rose (1984) is that governments before 1979 did not have much effect in shifting the macro-economic indicators, most of which steadily worsened from the 1950s. Rose argues that the record, from 1959 to 1979,

rejects a 'big bang' theory of parties making all the difference to Britain's government, let alone to society at large. But the record also shows that there are many *particular* differences in the way in which parties approach political problems and in the specific content and timing of a substantial amount of legislature. (1984, p. 151)

He suggests that the record is one of a 'moving consensus'.

Some commentators point to the failures of the Conservative Government since 1979 to reduce unemployment, or indeed to return to the level it inherited, or to cut back spending as a share of GDP, to refute claims that Thatcherism has made a difference. Just as we look back on the inter-war years as a period of missed opportunities in domestic and foreign policies, without differentiating between Baldwin, MacDonald and Chamberlain, so historians in the twenty-first century may well look back on the Wilson, Callaghan and Thatcher years of Britain's economic decline.

But this is to confuse policy outcome with policy choice and to adopt too narrow a focus. In so many fields – inflation, industrial relations, housing, home ownership, privatization of state-owned corporations, and the powers and role of local government, to name but a few – the Thatcher Governments, like those of Attlee, have for better or worse produced significant and intended changes of direction. The governmental records of *1945–51* and *post-1979* show that parties do make a difference. In both periods the delivery of new policies was supported by an alteration in the climate of opinion (which affected even opponents) and a sense that a change of direction was necessary. But political factors were also important.

Some of the conditions which serve to enhance the impact of party in government seem to be that a prime minister or group in the Cabinet: (a) has a clear sense of strategy (which this government, like that of Attlee, clearly has had); (b) is determined to succeed; (c) has control of the House of Commons; and (d) is prepared to weaken or even abolish institutions which obstruct the way. The British political system, characterized as it is by what Lord Hailsham has called the elective dictatorship of the executive, has undoubtedly helped the Thatcher Governments in producing the policy changes. Most other West European states have coalition governments, multi-party systems and proportional electoral systems. Elections in these states produce only modest shifts in seats and there is more continuity in government personnel. In Britain the electoral system translates modest swings in votes to big shifts in seats. Britain is one of the very few states where a single party wields the full panoply of power within the legislature. Parties do make a difference – and the difference can be seen both in the creation of the post-war consensus and in its subsequent partial destruction.

Afterword: From Thatcher to Major

The passage of four years since the book's first publication in 1989 provides a good opportunity to assess the validity of our original argument and take account of the departure of Mrs Thatcher and her replacement by John Major. *Consensus Politics* claimed that over the post-war period there were two discernible stages in the shaping of the policy agenda in Britain. The first covered the closing stages of the war-time coalition government, say from 1944, to the end of the 1945–1951 Labour governments. The second covered the period between 1979 and 1989, the years of the Thatcher governments. In both of these periods significant new initiatives were taken to shift the direction of existing policies. In 1951, the Conservatives returned to office and, notwithstanding their opposition during the previous six years to Labour policies, they accepted, albeit reluctantly, most of them. The period after 1951 to the mid-1970s has come to be regarded as a period of relatively consensual politics, in the sense of shared goals and means by the parties in government.

We insisted that the use of the term consensus does not preclude debate or differences between the parties over particular methods and timing of policies, as well as occasional policy reversals. Ironically, the latter were as likely to occur within the lifetime of a government as when there was a change of party in office. In the long-run, however, continuity was the order of the day in such areas as foreign affairs, defence, state provision of welfare, education and health, acceptance of a mixed economy, full employment and commitment to greater equality in life chances.

The 1980s saw a significant break with many elements of the post-war consensus. Indeed the break was so significant that many senior Conservatives protested at the change of direction. In repudiating much of the previous policy mix, Mrs Thatcher claimed that she was attempting to reverse the country's decline and was thus implicitly blaming her Conservative as well as Labour predecessors for presiding over policies which she believed contributed to that decline. Governments had too easily acquiesced in policies which devalued the currency and increased the powers of special interests. They were spending too much – and often doing it badly – and taxing too much. This was the Thatcherite critique of post-war Britain. A reduced role for government would give an opportunity for markets and the spirit of enterprise to flourish.

We are aware that some historians and political scientists have recently disputed the idea that there was such a thing as a post-war consensus. Jeffreys (1987) on social policy and Webster (1990) on the NHS in particular have claimed that the Attlee government's measures were not the product of agreement between the two major parties, and that many Conservatives in 1945 were deeply unhappy at the proposals. We do not regard this as a refutation of our thesis because our emphasis was on the continuity in government policy in these fields between 1951 and the 1970s. Pimlott (1988) claimed that for much of the post-war period the Labour and Conservative parties did not see themselves as practising consensus politics but thought that their battles involved serious disagreements of principle.

But, here again, what stands out is not the rhetoric of political controversy but the continuity in policy choice. It was not until 1979 that there was a serious and sustained attempt by the Thatcher government to shift the political agenda and one that was followed by an equivalent rejection of established policies by the Labour party. Our claim is that the temper of the party battle in the early 1980s was very different from that in the 1950s and 1960s (Kavanagh 1992).

Mrs Thatcher did not of course long survive the debate to

which she gave her name. Any assessment of the durability of her agenda must be highly tentative, for we can refer just to the three years of a Major government and the policies of the Labour opposition. Any review of significant political events since 1988, when we completed the first edition, will probably agree on the following:

1989	January	White Paper on NHS reforms (see below)
	May	Tenth anniversary of Mrs Thatcher's premiership
	October	Labour Conference approves multi-lateral disarmament – end of policy of unilateralism
1990	October	Britain joins ERM
	November	Sir Geoffrey Howe resigns
	November	Mrs Thatcher resigns: succeeded by John Major
1991	April	Labour policy changes, following the Policy Review
	July	Citizen's Charter
	December	Maastricht; Britain opts out of Social Charter and EMU
1992	April	General Election: fourth consecutive Conservative victory
	June	John Smith succeeds Neil Kinnock as Labour leader
	September	Britain forced to leave ERM
1993		Announcement of plans for semi-privatization of British Rail.

The Policy Agenda Post-1988

Welfare

Traditionally, welfare has been seen as Labour's favoured ground because that party has been associated by the public with a willingness to spend more on social security, education and health. Conservatives are associated with a greater tolerance of private provision of, for example, pensions, education and health, more support for selectivity of benefits, and seeking value for money. Across many social policy areas the Conservatives, since 1987, have adopted a rhetoric of promoting 'standards' and 'choice', to be achieved by privatization, the contracting out of services, increasing competition and the scope of the market, and publishing consumers' and customers' charters. This approach has accelerated under John Major. And since the election defeat of 1992, Labour, although still emphasising the virtues of public provision, has adopted some of this rhetoric and appears to be embracing some of these policies.

No area of the welfare system has been exempt from change. The Education Reform Act (1988) made the most far-reaching reforms to the school system since the 1944 Education Act. It introduced testing of school pupils at the age of 7, allowed schools to opt out of local authority control and head teachers to manage their own budgets, and imposed a core 'national' curriculum. It also introduced loans for students in higher education while freezing student maintenance grants at their current level. In 1991 health hospitals were allowed to become self-governing trusts and doctors in large practices were encouraged to apply to manage their own budgets; an internal market was established in which hospitals competed for patients on the basis of their services and costs. Doctors could now purchase services for patients from trust hospitals or their own directly managed hospitals.

In its 1992 election manifesto Labour promised to return the opted-out hospitals to local NHS authorities and end the internal market. Since the 1992 election defeat Labour health spokesmen have shown signs of accepting these changes. Conservative ministers have been sensitive to opposition charges that they planned to privatize the welfare state and have avoided such radical free market ideas as education vouchers or significantly extending private health care, and remained committed to financing the health and education systems overwhelmingly out of taxation.

In many Western countries the slowdown of economic

growth, rising unemployment and an elderly population are imposing strains on public spending – particularly on the social security and health budgets. In the 1990s it is not only the political right which wonders whether the stubborn problems of poverty and deprivation require a new look at universal schemes of welfare provision. In the Labour party, speeches by David Blunkett and Frank Field have reflected an appreciation of the case for more targeting of benefits, both to tackle severe hardship and curb the demands on the public purse. Influenced by President-elect Clinton's proposals for 'workfare' – i.e. a person's entitlement to benefit entails an obligation to seek and prepare for employment – they have argued that any welfare policy should not only protect the poor and the weak but also seek to make people more self-reliant. In retrospect, a number of Labour leaders have claimed that the party's proposals to increase the income tax burden on the better off – required to fund promised uprating in universal old age pensions and child benefits – contributed to its fourth election defeat in 1992. Might the party's new commission on social justice broaden the debate to include more selectivity and targeting? All parties are likely to re-examine the relevance of the Beveridge welfare state in a society which has changed greatly since Beveridge's scheme was drawn up. That scheme assumed relatively full employment, most wives remaining at home, and stable two-parent families.

Industrial Relations

Here is an issue on which the agenda has changed decisively since 1979. In the 1970s the power of the trade unions to break incomes policies was widely seen as a challenge to Parliament and commentators wondered how – and sometimes whether – our political institutions might cope with the power of the producer interests. But by the time Mrs Thatcher left office the wings of the unions had been severely clipped; talk of the need for 'contracts' between government and the interests for effective policy making, of incomes policies for tackling inflation or of union vetoes on policies were a thing of the past. A legal framework had been established which limited the powers and autonomy of the unions. After 1987 Labour made substantial moves to accept the more popular elements, including the end of the closed shop, pre-strike ballots and election of union officials by members. Defenders of the reforms claimed that they had helped to strengthen management, reduce the number of days lost to strikes and produced a more flexible workforce. The Labour party has agreed to reduce the size of the trade union block vote at the annual conference and moved to a one member one vote system in the selection of candidates; this will further dilute trade union influence.

Elsewhere, some differences between the parties remain, notably on the European Community's Social Charter, which gives employees more rights at work. The Conservatives will not accept it, on the grounds that it increases the costs to employers and damages employment prospects. Labour backs the Charter and it was a significant factor in the party's growing enthusiasm for Europe. Labour's proposed minimum wage remains another area of difference between the parties. An echo of the 1970s was the Labour party's 1992 manifesto promise of an annual national economic assessment, which would influence collective bargaining between 'employers, trade unions and other social partners'. Labour still appeared to think of workplace rights being exercised through and by trade unions, rather than individuals, and rejected the sanction of possible seizure of trade union assets by the courts, when unions broke the law.

The Mixed Economy

During the first Thatcher government Labour had opposed the government's privatization measures. By 1988, however, it was clear that it had abandoned any thoughts of a return to nationalization, although it opposed the additional privatization of water in 1989 and electricity in 1990, as well as Conservative plans to privatize coal and parts of the railway system in the longer term. But it was notable that Labour no longer regarded re-nationalization of the privatized companies as a priority or preached the benefits of the old Morrison-style nationalization. There were no votes to be gained by going back to the

policies of 1945; the nationalized industries had few supporters. Instead, the party placed more emphasis on the need
for greater regulation and competition within the privatized
monopolies and more public accountability. Its 1989 policy
statement *Meet the Challenge. Make the Change* stated that a future
Labour government would work with a successful market
economy and that state intervention should be limited to areas
where the market was failing, for example, in investment and
training. Since 1979 the boundary between the public and
private sectors of the economy has been redrawn, with some
two-thirds of those formerly state owned undertakings being
privatized.

Britain's poor economic performance on jobs, growth and
balance of payments has destroyed the claims that the
Thatcher decade – and its free market policies – produced an
'economic miracle'. There has developed an awareness of the
limits of the free market, and in early 1993 the government was
forced by public clamour to reverse for a time proposals to
close a number of coal mines. The new Secretary of State at the
DTI, Michael Heseltine, believes that any modern government
should have an industrial strategy and be prepared to intervene. But the new consensus on the primacy of the market is
very different from that of the 1970s.

Full Employment

At the time of our first edition, unemployment was becoming a
less pressing problem. By July 1988 the jobless total had fallen
to 2.3 million or 7.5 per cent of the workforce, the 24th con-
secutive month in which the unemployment figures had fallen.
The totals continued to fall to 1.6 million and 5.7 per cent by
the middle of 1990. Both figures were of course higher than
had been the case for the first thirty post-war years but were a
considerable improvement on the figures prevailing during
most of the 1980s. Thereafter, however, the figures steadily
rose to near 10 per cent and almost three million by the end of
1992. The acceptance by both parties of Britain's membership
of the ERM from October 1990 restricted any governments'
ability to pursue active employment policies, to lower interest

rates or increase borrowing. During 1992 criticism grew of British membership of the ERM and pursuit of the policy goal of very low inflation at virtually any cost. But the leadership of the major parties appeared committed to the policy. The forced withdrawal of Britain from the ERM in September 1992 gave renewed respectability to Keynesian ideas and increased the number of voices calling for government intervention, more public spending on infrastructure and, a particular demand of Labour's, greater training and investment. Although all major parties have policies for improving the working of the economy, for economic growth and for the creation of more jobs, the pursuit of a full employment policy – say a target of unemployment of 3 per cent or less, and a set of policies which would achieve this – has been set aside since the mid 1970s.

Foreign Policy

Foreign policy has been mainly concerned with the European Community. The dissolution of the USSR in 1991 and the end of the Cold War instantly removed defence as an issue. British membership of the EC is no longer a divide between the parties, though they are divided, as we have seen, over whether Britain should return to the ERM, and implementing the Maastricht Treaty. It is interesting to note how the Euro-sceptics, found largely on the Conservative benches, have echoed the rhetoric of the old anti-marketeers. They resist further convergence of British with European policies, and defend the nation state against a European superstate and a sovereign House of Commons against the Brussels Commission. In her speech at Bruges in September 1988, Mrs Thatcher made clear her attachment to British sovereignty:

We have not rolled back the frontiers of the state in Britain to see them reimposed at a European level with a European superstate exercising a new dominance from Brussels!

On defence, we have noted that Labour's adoption of a uni-lateral defence policy not only broke the post-war consensus, but made defence an important issue in the 1983 and 1987 elections, disastrously so for Labour. Thereafter, Mr Kinnock gradually edged away from unilateralism and its abandonment was formally confirmed at the 1989 party conference. This policy shift, combined with the breakup of the Soviet Empire, resulted in the relegation of defence as an issue in the 1992 general election.

The Role of the Opposition

Our conclusion to the first edition raised the question of whether Mrs Thatcher had changed the political agenda in such a way that her policies would survive her departure from the political scene (p. 123). Any answer to this question would necessarily have to wait until the records of at least one successor non-Conservative government or a post-Thatcher Conservative government could be examined. It has often been observed that the crucial test for new constitutions, institutions and programmes is their ability to outlive their founders. It was clear, for example, that by 1959, after eight years of Conservative rule, many of the policies of the 1945 Labour government – the nationalized industries, the NHS, the commitment to full employment, the membership of the Atlantic Alliance and the evolution of Europe into a Commonwealth – were common ground.

Because there has not yet been a post-Thatcher Labour government, one is reduced to examining Labour's policies in opposition. We noted that by 1987 the Labour party had already moved away from the left-wing manifesto it produced for the 1983 election – one that promised a 35-hour working week, import controls, price controls, sweeping measures of public ownership and compulsory planning agreements with private companies, the repeal of recent employment legislation, unilateral British abandonment of nuclear weapons, and withdrawal from the European Community. The shift of direction was confirmed in the party's extended Policy Review between 1988 and 1990. The review was part of a larger project to make Labour electable and in particular to slough off its association with unpopular policies, notably high taxes, nationalization, the trade unions and the loony left (Hughes and Wintour, 1990). As part of this refurbishing of Labour's image the new policies included:

- the abandonment of unilateral disarmament: Britain would retain nuclear weapons until they were negotiated away in multilateral talks;
- no wholesale re-nationalization of privatized corporations, although measures would be taken to increase regulation and competition in the privatized utilities;
- acceptance of the end of the closed shop, pre-strike ballots and the election of union executives. However, there would be the restoration of limited secondary action and no sequestration of trade union funds;
- no target for reducing unemployment;
- limitation of public spending to what Britain could afford;
- acceptance of membership of the European Community and Labour would go further than the Conservatives, in accepting the Social Charter and membership of the EMS.

These shifts in policy meant that many of the battles of the 1970s and early 1980s, including those over membership of the European Community, nuclear weapons, council house sales and privatization were effectively over. There was now much common ground between the parties. Labour had effectively abandoned state socialism and even large scale redistribution, and accepted that markets were superior to state planning in creating wealth. Labour leaders made friendly noises about the virtues of markets, viewed the state as a partner for business and, in the words of the 1992 manifesto, promised 'A government that business can do business with'. Crushing election defeats had killed off state socialism. But the left was also a casualty of the globalization of the British economy, which meant that planning the economy on a national scale was no longer practical politics. Membership of the European Community imposed constraints upon what any government could do to manage its own economy. Ivor Crewe (1990) regards the shift from the 1983 and 1987 manifestos not so much as an acceptance of Thatcherism but of the programme of the breakaway Social Democratic Party, formed by Labour right-wingers in 1981.

Some areas of disagreement between the major parties remained. One was constitutional reform. Labour was committed to examining the merits of proportional representation and was pledged to greater devolution for the regions, fixed term parliaments, a charter of rights, a Scottish Assembly and an elected second chamber. But elsewhere how much of a divide was there? On health it promised improvements, largely through the provision of greater resources. On education it would end opting out of local authority control, assisted places, the 11+ and student loans. Again there was the promise of more spending; but only as resources allowed. In addition, local management of budgets and a core curriculum would remain. And by the end of 1992 the party seemed to be backing off its election proposals on taxation and public spending.

We originally claimed that decisive shifts in the policy agenda occurred as a result of the interaction of three factors: personality – the goals and values of politicians in key positions; circumstances – the need for solutions to pressing problems; ideas – the climate of opinion about realistic and desirable policy goals and the means of achieving them. These factors combined in the 1940s and again in the 1980s to produce a sense that existing policies were failing and that new ones could do better. What is crucial is that all these factors are in place, although there may be disagreement about their relative importance at different points in the reform stage. In a recent essay Anthony King (1992) has assessed the reasons for Mrs Thatcher's ability to overthrow the old agenda. He is not impressed with the impact of the civil service, party doctrine, public opinion or interest groups but prefers to emphasise the changing climate of ideas, or what he calls 'thoughts in politicians heads'. And ideas once established can generate ways to consolidate themselves. Once contracting out, privatization and devolved budgets to schools or doctors are established, they build constituencies to support them. King also has no doubt of the key importance of Mrs Thatcher, stating that 'She was the prime mover' in shaping the new agenda (42).

Many factors influence the decision of an opposition party to abandon or modify a policy. They may include calculations about its financial costs or administrative practicality, pressure from public opinion, interest groups or party activists, preferences of key policymakers and spokesmen, changes in the real world, and so on. More than anything else the scale of the party's electoral rebuff in 1983 and 1987 was decisive in encouraging Labour to change policies. These were the party's worst results since 1931; the supposed party of the working class gained the support of less than half of the workers. In both elections, the not unrealistic goal of the new Alliance was to overtake Labour as the second most popular party. Whereas previous election defeats had usually seen the party turn to the left, after 1983 and more so after 1987 the party leadership adapted to the agenda set by the Conservatives.

The 1992 election defeat – particularly the margin in popular votes – came as a shock to Labour leaders. The opinion polls had provided reassurance during the campaign, Labour benefited from the mood for change following thirteen years of Conservative rule, and the economic recession damaged Conservative claims to economic competence and increased popular dissatisfaction with the government. Yet, against the odds, the Conservatives won again. Fear of Labour, particularly doubts about its economic competence, seemed a stronger negative force than dissatisfaction with the government. After the 1992 election it seemed that the party would have to change even more. Post-election surveys conducted for the party suggested that Labour lost because it was no longer speaking even for many of its natural supporters in the working class. People were aspirational, they wanted more material goods and regarded Labour as a party that was 'dragging down' and 'holding back' those who strived to better themselves.

The Impact of Major

A cyclical view sees history moving through recurring patterns, of ebbs and flows, times of radical reform followed by times of consolidation, of radical reformist leaders, followed by more cautious ones. There is no doubt that Mrs Thatcher was, and intended to be, a disturber of existing policies and of many institutions and ideas. This was so much the case that some doubted that she was a Conservative at all. Although she differed in many respects from Heath, Macmillan and the One National Conservatives who dominated the leadership, the party has long included a free market individualist strand. Mrs Thatcher represented the re-assertion of the latter, although the former has prevailed for most of the twentieth century, particularly when the party was in office. On this reading the Major leadership in the 1990s will see a consolidation of earlier policies rather than new initiatives and will also act as a corrective to the path-breaking 1980s. There will be an awareness of the limits of markets and acceptance of a more active role for the state.

Many factors led to Mrs Thatcher's fall from the premiership (Anderson, 1991, Watkins, 1991). They included the unpopularity of the poll tax (widely regarded as her tax), her hostility to the European Community which not only offended the pro-Europeans in the party but was destabilizing the Cabinet, the conviction of many MPs that they could not win an election under her, as well as the long-standing opposition of anti-Thatcherites in the party. But just as it would be wrong to interpret the various factors which led the Conservative MPs to vote for Mrs Thatcher rather than Ted Heath as leader in 1975 as an endorsement of 'Thatcherism', so it would be too much to say that her failure to win the leadership election was a repudiation of Thatcherism. Ideology was only a minor element in her rise and her fall.

John Major clearly differs from Mrs Thatcher in the sense of not being dynamic, dogmatic, dismissive of other views, and determined to offer leadership by conviction. But he has been concerned to distinguish himself from his predecessor. His election was helped by the fact that many Conservative MPs regarded him as the candidate most likely to keep the party together and to win the general election, but part of his appeal to the right of the party was that he was also more likely than Douglas Hurd or Michael Heseltine, the rival candidates for the leadership, to carry on her work. His government has provided continuity on privatization, trade union reforms and the commitment to lower income tax, but responded to the mood which led to her departure by replacing the poll tax, uprating child benefit and adopting a more conciliatory tone with the European Community.

As Prime Minister, John Major also showed himself to be more interested in tapping the views of the Cabinet, in consulting it and maintaining its unity. This has been particularly true on the European Community, notably leading up to Maastricht, on replacing the poll tax with a council tax, on reversing the plans to dismantle the coal industry, and in preparing the 1992 election manifesto. Mrs Thatcher had set more of a lead to Cabinet and on the first two issues sought to impose her views on increasingly uneasy colleagues. Perhaps influenced by the rhetoric of 'Thatcherism' some commentators spent time trying to define Majorism. Mrs Thatcher cuttingly remarked that there was no such thing as 'Majorism' and John Major discouraged such a search. In this respect he suffered from comparison with his predecessor, but it was probably inevitable that any successor to Mrs Thatcher would appear to lack conviction and vision. The Citizen's Charter is very much his idea and the themes of promoting a 'classless society' by extending opportunities for greater choice and ownership recur through his speeches.

The End of Ideology Again?

In an echo of the 'end of ideology' debate of the 1950s and early 1960s, many commentators have argued that programmatic politics based on alternative principled programmes has ended. Britain is in a post-Thatcher, post-socialist era. More generally, Francis Fukuyama's *The End of History* (1990) proclaims the victory of liberal democracy and capitalist economics, following the collapse of Communism in Eastern Europe. The British Labour party's retreats on policy and defeats in elections have been paralleled by the failure of the left in most of Western Europe in recent years to offer distinctive election winning policies. One indicator of the new thinking on the left was the lecture by one of the foremost thinkers of the liberal left, the American economist J. K. Galbraith, at the Institute of Public Policy in November 1992. His call for rethinking involved a dismissal of ideology. He said that the new left must adapt to

. . . an age of constructive pragmatism. Issues must be decided on their merits. There can be no escape from thought into theology. Thus our attitude to public ownership. We are not committed to it in principle any more than we accept the theologically based conservative commitment to privatisation. We are for what works best. Similarly, there is no general case for or against government intervention. Here, too, decision must be on social merits.

John Major was as likely as Neil Kinnock or John Smith to say 'Amen' to that.

Bibliography

Addison, P. (1975) *The Road to 1945* (London, Cape).

Allen, V. (1960) *Trade Unions and the Government* (London, Longman).

Anderson, B. (1991) *John Major: the making of the Prime Minister* (London, Fourth Estates).

Bacon, R. and Eltis, W. (1976) *Britain's Economic Problems: Too Few Producers* (London, Macmillan).

Barnes, D. and Reid, E. (1980) *Governments and the Trade Unions* (London, Heinemann).

Barnett, C. (1986) *The Audit of War* (London, Macmillan).

Barnett, J. (1982) *Inside the Treasury* (London, Deutsch).

Beer, S. (1969) *Modern British Politics* (London, Faber).

Beer, S. (1982) *Britain Against Itself* (London, Faber).

Birkenhead, Lord (1969) *Walter Monckton: The Life of Viscount Monckton of Brenchley* (London, Weidenfeld and Nicolson).

Bogdanor, V. (1983) 'Lions and Ostriches', *Encounter*, July.

British Social Attitudes: The 1987 Report (1988) (London, Gower Press).

Brittan, S. (1971) *Steering the Economy* (Harmondsworth, Penguin).

Brittan, S. (1975) 'The Economic Contradictions of Democracy', *British Journal of Political Science*. Vol. V.

Budge, I., Robertson, D. and Rallings, C. (1987) *Ideology, Strategy and Party Change* (Cambridge, Cambridge University Press).

Cameron, D. (1983) 'Social Democracy, Corporatism, Labour Acquiescence and the Representation of Economic Interests in Advanced Capitalist Society' in J. Goldthorpe (ed.) *Order and Conflict in Contemporary Capitalism* (Oxford, Clarendon Press).

Chapman, B. (1963) *British Government Observed* (London, Allen and Unwin).

Crewe, I. (1990) 'The Policy Agenda' *Contemporary Record*, February.

Crosland, A. (1956) *The Future of Socialism* (London, Cape).

Eden, A. (1960) *Full Circle* (London, Cassell).

Finer, S. E. (1975) *Adversary Politics and Electoral Reform* (London, Wigram).

Fisher, N. (1973) *Ian Macleod* (London, Deutsch).

Frankel, J. (1975) *British Foreign Policy* (Oxford, Oxford University Press).

Fukuyama, F. (1990) *The End of History and the Last Man* (London, Hamish Hamilton).

Gamble, A. (1974) *The Conservative Nation* (London, Routledge).

Gamble, A. and Walkland, S. (1984) *The British Party System and Economic Policy* (Oxford, Clarendon Press).

Gilbert, B. (1970) *British Social Policy 1914–1939* (London, Batsford).

Gilmour, I. (1983) *Britain Can Work* (Oxford, Martin Robertson).

Goldsworthy, D. (1971) *Colonial Issues and British Politics 1945–61* (Oxford, Oxford University Press).

Goodman, G. (1979) *The Awkward Warrior: Frank Cousins, His Life and Times* (London, Davis-Poynter).

Greenleaf, W. H. (1987) *The British Political Tradition* Vol. III Part I (London, Methuen).

Halsey, A., Heath, A. and Ridge, J. (1979) *Origins and Destinations* (Oxford, Clarendon Press).

Heald, D. (1983) *Public Expenditure* (Oxford, Martin Robertson).

Heath, A., Jowell, R. and Curtice, J. (1985) *How Britain Votes* (Oxford, Pergamon).

Hennessy, P. and Seldon, A. (1987) *Ruling Performance* (Oxford, Blackwell).

Hoffman, S. (1964) *The Conservative Party in Opposition* (London, McGibbon and Kee).

Hogg, Q. (1974) *The Case for Conservatism* (Harmondsworth, Penguin).

Holland, S. (1975) *The Challenge of Socialism* (London, Quartet).

Holmes, M. and Horsewood, N. (1988) 'The Post-War Consensus', *Contemporary Record* Vol. 2 No. 2, Summer.

Hughes, C. and Wintour, P. (1990) *Labour Rebuilt* (London, Fourth Estates).

Jeffreys, K. (1987) 'British Politics and Social Policy During the Second World War', *Historical Journal*, Vol. 30, No. 1, pp. 123–44.

Jenkins, P. (1987) *Mrs Thatcher's Revolution* (London, Cape).

Joseph, K. (1975) *Reversing the Trend* (London, Barry Rose).

Kavanagh, D. (1987) *Thatcherism and British Politics* (Oxford, Oxford University Press).

Kavanagh, D. (1992) 'Debate. The Post-War Consensus' *Twentieth Century British History*, Vol. 3, No. 2, pp. 175–90.

Keynes, J. (1936) *The General Theory of Employment, Interest and Money* (London, Macmillan).

King, A. (1973) 'Ideas, Institutions and the Policies of Government: A Comparative Analysis', *British Journal of Political Science* Vol. III.

King, A. (1992) 'Political Change in Britain', in D. Kavanagh (ed.) *Electoral Politics* (Oxford, Oxford University Press).

Kitzinger, Y. (1973) *Diplomacy and Persuasion: How Britain Joined the Common Market* (London, Thames and Hudson).

Klein, R. (1983) *The Politics of the National Health Service* (London, Longman).

Klein, R. and O'Higgins, M. (1985) *The Future of Welfare* (Oxford, Blackwell).

Le Grand, J. (1982) *The Strategy of Equality* (London, Allen and Unwin).

MacGregor, S. (1981) *The Politics of Poverty* (London, Longman).

Marquand, D. (1988a) *The Unprincipled Society* (London, Cape).

Marquand, D. (1988b) 'Post-War Consensus and its Decline', *Contemporary Record* Vol. 2 No. 3, Autumn.

Matthews, R. (1968) 'Why has Britain had Full Employment Since the War?', *Economic Journal* Vol. 78.

McKenzie, R. (1955) *British Political Parties* (London, Heinemann).

Middlemas, K. (1979) *The Politics of Industrial Society* (London, Deutsch).

Miliband, R. (1961) *Parliamentary Socialism* (London, Allen and Unwin).

Miliband, R. (1969) *The State in Capitalist Society* (London, Weidenfeld and Nicolson).

Moran, M. (1977) *The Politics of Industrial Relations* (London, Macmillan).

Morgan, K. (1985) *Labour in Power* (Oxford, Oxford University Press).

Mowat, C. (1955) *Britain Between the Wars* (London, Methuen).

O'Connor, J. (1973) *The Fiscal Crisis of the Capitalist State* (New York, St Martins).

Pelling, H. (1970) *Britain and the Second World War* (London, Collins).

Pelling, H. (1971) *The History of British Trade Unionism* (Harmondsworth, Penguin).

Phillips, W. A. (1958) 'The Relationship between Unemployment and the Rate of Change of Money Wages in the United Kingdom, 1861–1957', *Economica* Vol. 25.

Pierre, A. (1972) *Nuclear Politics: The British Experience with an Independent Strategic Force 1939—70* (Oxford, Oxford University Press).

Pimlott, B. (1988) 'The Myth of Consensus' in L. M. Smith (ed.) *The Making of Britain: Echoes of Greatness* (London, Macmillan).

Pliatzky, L. (1984) *Getting and Spending* (Oxford, Blackwell).

Pryke, R. (1981) *The Nationalised Industries* (Oxford, Martin Robertson).

Rose, R. (1976) 'On the Priorities of Government', *European Journal of Political Research* Vol. 4.

Rose, R. (1984) *Do Parties Make a Difference?* 2nd edition (London, Macmillan).

Rose, R. (1985) *Politics in England* 4th edition (London, Faber).

Rose, R. and Peters, G. (1978) *Can Government Go Bankrupt?* (London, Macmillan).

Seldon, A. (1981) *Churchill's Indian Summer* (London, Hodder and Stoughton).

Seldon, A. (1985) (ed.) *The New Enlightenment* (London, Institute of Economic Affairs).

Shonfield, A. (1965) *Modern Capitalism* (Oxford, Oxford University Press).

Skidelsky, R. (1977) (ed.) *The End of the Keynesian Era* (London, Macmillan).

Stewart, M. (1978) *Politics and Economic Policy in the United Kingdom Since 1964* (Oxford, Pergamon).

Taylor, R. (1987) 'Trade Unions since 1945: Scapegoats of Economic Decline', *Contemporary Record* Vol. I, No. 2, Summer.

Watkins, A. (1991) *A Conservative Coup: the fall of Margaret Thatcher* (London, Duckworth).

Webster, C. (1988) 'Origins of the NHS', *Contemporary Record* Vol. II, No. 2, Summer.

Webster, C. (1990) 'Conflict and Consensus: Explaining the British Health Service' *Twentieth Century British History*, Vol. 1, No. 2, pp. 115–51.

Worcester, R. (1988) 'Polls Apart', *New Socialist*, Summer.

Index